EMPOWERING STUDENTS *With* TECHNOLOGY

Second Edition

EMPOWERING STUDENTS *With* TECHNOLOGY

Second Edition

ALAN NOVEMBER

CORWIN
A SAGE Company

For information:

Corwin
A SAGE Company
2455 Teller Road
Thousand Oaks, California 91320
(800) 233-9936
Fax: (800) 417-2466
www.corwinpress.com

SAGE Ltd.
1 Oliver's Yard
55 City Road
London EC1Y 1SP
United Kingdom

SAGE India Pvt. Ltd.
B 1/I 1 Mohan Cooperative
   Industrial Area
Mathura Road, New Delhi 110 044
India

SAGE Asia-Pacific Pte. Ltd.
33 Pekin Street #02-01
Far East Square
Singapore 048763

Printed in the United States of America

Library of Congress Cataloging-in-Publication Data

November, Alan C.
Empowering students with technology/Alan November.—2nd ed.
    p. cm.
Includes bibliographical references and index.
ISBN 978-1-4129-7425-7 (pbk.)

   1. Computer-assisted instruction—United States. 2. Internet in education—United States. 3. Educational innovations—United States. I. National Association of Secondary School Principals (U.S.) II. Title.

LB1028.43.N69 2010
371.33´40973—dc22   2009043649

This book is printed on acid-free paper.

              11   12   13   10   9   8   7   6   5   4   3

Acquisitions Editor:	Hudson Perigo
Associate Editor:	Julie McNall
Production Editor:	Amy Schroller
Copy Editor:	Jenifer Dill
Typesetter:	C&M Digitals (P) Ltd.
Proofreader:	Victoria Reed-Castro
Indexer:	Nara Wood
Cover Designer:	Anthony Paular
Graphic Designer:	Rose Storey

Contents

Preface

About 30 years ago, one of my high school students, Yves, profoundly changed my vision of education and helped me to understand how technology can be used to motivate students to learn. Yves broke into the computer lab on a Friday after school, and as director of the alternative high school, it was my job to deliver the discipline. Before Yves' adventure, I was happily teaching social studies and had never even touched a computer. Yves had been branded as a classic underachiever. He consistently demonstrated poor classroom performance (despite fairly good test scores) and sporadic school attendance. In fact, the computer lab break-in occurred 10 days before his classmates were scheduled to graduate without him.

When I walked into the computer lab, it was foreign territory to me—in 1981, all computers were owned by the math department. But there Yves sat, busily striking the Chiclet-like keys on the Commodore Pet computer. An audiotape drive was plugged into the back of the computer, but I was surprised—where was the music? In those days there was no software. Computers did not come with disk drives. All you could do with a computer was write your own programs and then record the information on an audiotape. Yves had been busy recording a program of his own making.

I was not prepared for the direction of the conversation with Yves. He explained that he did not break in to do anything wrong; instead, he wanted to see how well he could write computer code. The alleged need to discipline a student was quickly replaced by the need to help a student gain access to academic resources that could help him graduate.

Yves offered to show me what he was doing. He took me to a computer and ran several of the programming sequences he had developed. I did not have a clue what I was looking at, but I could decipher this much: he knew exactly what he was doing, and it interested him beyond belief. I was shocked. In 10 years of working with at-risk students, none had ever broken into an academic area to do work. I was fascinated by his fascination.

The second stunning revelation came when he said, without pause, "I could do this whole course in a weekend." He wasn't bragging (well, maybe a little); he was stating a fact. Here was a kid who, in all likelihood, was not going to graduate because he didn't have enough credits (classes bored him), and he was claiming to be able to do a computer programming course in a weekend at the end of the school year. How could he?

I was still soaking in the fact that he did not deserve punishment for what he had done when he repeated, "If you can arrange for me to take home a computer, I could come back on Monday with the work finished." We talked for a while. Maybe he could. . . .

Later that afternoon, I went to the math teacher who, like math teachers all over the United States in the early 1980s, was in charge of the computer lab. I told him I thought we should give Yves the chance to do what he said he could do—complete the programming course. It would give him the credits he needed to graduate. "No way," was the somewhat predictable reply. I pressed on: "Let's send the computer home with him over the weekend and see what he can do. What have we got to lose?" Wrong question. "We could lose the computer," he said, amazed at my naiveté. Finally, after some negotiation with the principal and Yves' mom, we boxed up the equipment and sent Yves home for the weekend. It was like sending a kid home with a basketball and a hoop. To Yves it was a game, and he understood how to improve his skills.

Yves arrived Monday morning with all the computer programming course work done, and done well—a slam dunk! The only part that disappointed me was the grade Yves' earned: a *C*. Since he had not actually attended any of the programming classes, he was marked down for not coming to class. Yves did not care about the grade. He had proved he was capable of doing the work. He did it without the rigorous structure of a standard classroom. No attendance, no grades, no 45-minute periods, no homework, no teacher monitoring daily what he was doing. As Mihaly Csikszentmihalyi (1991) would say, "He was into the flow of an optimal experience." Previously, the system had locked Yves into a pattern of failure, and he literally had to break in to break away from it. The ironic thing is that the same system rewarded him with graduation, told him he had done good work, and sent him out into the world. He went on to earn both a bachelor's and a master's degree.

Yves graduated by virtue of his breaking and entering, and I began a journey that still motivates me today. At first, my goal was simply to understand the fascination and focus that many students have with technology. But now, I find myself exploring ways to reorganize the culture of learning to take advantage of students' natural desire to explore their world and to develop the skills that are needed to solve increasingly complex problems. Yves not only sat down with me and showed me how computers worked, he also taught me something even more important: technology can be a powerful motivator for some students who do not succeed in traditional classrooms. At the core of Yves' motivation and focus was a shift of control regarding who manages learning. Even though he was downgraded for not coming to class, Yves took pride and possession of his own learning, and the faceless programming machine gave him the environment of instant feedback. Yves showed me that as soon as you write a program, you can test it; the computer lets you know if you need to continue to work on it. Instant feedback can help students remain focused and work through problems. The other quality the computer has is a total lack of judgment. It does not care how often the learner makes a mistake. The dehumanized environment of the computer can actually create a very healthy learning environment for some students, especially for at-risk students. This is one of the reasons why online learning will explode. The anonymity of the Internet provides this same lack of judgment and, if designed correctly, provides instant feedback.

In the nearly 30 years since I was sent to punish Yves for breaking into the computer lab, I have watched for other examples of this shift in the control of learning. As our learning technologies have become more sophisticated, I have witnessed numerous examples. While a real fear exists that we are losing students to the computer and that increased computer use will erode face-to-face social skills, there is the upside potential of empowering students to have the confidence and the courage to learn without needing the formal structure of the traditional classroom.

Indeed, I now see the real revolution in learning as a greater sense of freedom to access information and people with powerful tools. In many ways, the ability of students to manage this learning mirrors the emerging skill set of the knowledge economy, where increasing numbers of workers are given the freedom to manage their own work. Increasingly, the new economy requires workers to be self-directed, self-assessing, and interdependent.

However, adding technology to the classroom is the easy part. The difficult work is reshaping the relationship between teachers and students. The real revolution in learning is not about adding technology on top of the current structure of schooling. Instead, the real revolution is about a transformational shift of control from the school system to the learner. Teachers are faced with the historic opportunity of teaching students to know what to do with their power to access unlimited amounts of information and to extend their relationships of learning. We are embarking on a journey where the traditional boundaries of schooling are likely to be challenged and redesigned. If we are up to the task, many more students will be empowered to see learning as an adventure.

At an education conference in England, an insightful teacher made this distinction between what our schools were designed to do and what we need to do: "We have succeeded at teaching our students how to be taught, and what we need to do is to teach them how to learn."

This book explores the unique opportunities that technology provides to empower students to learn how to learn. It builds on the work of many pioneering educators who are breaking the traditional boundaries of learning. Enjoy. It is a very exciting time to be in education.

Alan November
Marblehead, MA
2010

A note to readers:

Please do not hesitate to get in touch with me to share your own stories and activities to help students make meaning of the world.

E-mail me at alan@novemberlearning.com or visit www.novemberlearning .com to learn more about activities and ideas.

—*Alan November*

Acknowledgments

I would like to gratefully acknowledge the following people:

My assistant, Lelia Richardson, who made sure that the details were done; Sheila Watson, formerly of Apple, who supported my work with students with grants; Bob Pearlman, who urged me to think about restructuring; Earle Hancock of Minuteman Tech in Lexington, Massachusetts, who taught me the joy of working with teachers; Lee Ann Potter, from the National Archives, who taught me to value authentic documents; Chris Dede, from Harvard, who taught me to think in the future and work backwards; David Barr, from the Illinois Math and Science Academy, who taught me to shift perspective to information literacy; Holly Brady, from Stanford, who provided the guidance and support to bring powerful ideas together in one place; Geoff Strack, from London, England, and Bridget Somekh, from Cambridge, England, who pushed me to think globally and critically; the teachers and staff of Pioneering Partners, who shared some of the most amazing stories of students who can achieve far beyond our current expectations.

About the Author

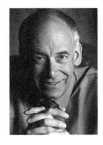 **Alan November** is an international leader in education technology. He began his career as an oceanography teacher and dorm counselor at an island reform school for boys in Boston Harbor. He has been director of an alternative high school, computer coordinator, technology consultant, and university lecturer. He has helped schools, governments, and industry leaders improve the quality of education through technology.

Audiences enjoy Alan's humor and wit as he pushes the boundaries of how to improve teaching and learning. His areas of expertise include planning across curriculum, staff development, new school design, community building, and leadership development. He has delivered keynotes and workshops in all fifty states, across Canada, and throughout the UK, Europe, Asia, and Central America.

Alan was named one of the nation's fifteen most influential thinkers of the decade by *Classroom Computer Learning Magazine.* In 2001, he was listed one of eight educators to provide leadership into the future by the Eisenhower National Clearinghouse. In 2007 he was selected to speak at the Cisco Public Services Summit during the Nobel Prize Festivities in Stockholm, Sweden. His writing includes numerous articles and a best-selling book, *Empowering Students With Technology.* Alan was co-founder of the Stanford Institute for Educational Leadership Through Technology and is most proud of being selected as one of the original five national Christa McAuliffe Educators.

Each summer Alan leads the Building Learning Communities summer conference with world-class presenters and participants from all over the world. Visit novemberlearning.com/blc for more details.

*To Dad, who taught me to continuously
explore big ideas and was proud of me for becoming a teacher.*

Introduction

CRAFTING A VISION FOR EMPOWERING STUDENTS

For the past 30 years, the promise of increasing processing power, quantum leaps in storage, nearly unlimited bandwidth, and the shrinking of computers into handheld devices has caused many educators to dream about the potential of harnessing this power to improve learning. Technology is finally faster, cheaper, easier, and smaller. How long will it take to convert this amazing change in technology into improved learning? Will we have 10 times the learning with 10 times the processing speed? What is the formula for converting megahertz, RAM, and megabits into learning results? What can we realistically expect the impact of technology on learning to be?

The nation is continuing to pour money into educational technology programs. Quality Education Data, Inc., the Denver-based education market-research firm, forecasted in 2004 that public schools in the United States would spend upwards of $7 billion, or $140.31 per student, on technology during the 2004–2005 school year. This number is up from the $5.67 billion reportedly spent just five years ago. With the cost of purchasing individual computers dropping at a tremendous rate, this number is even more impressive. As a nation, we are placing technology in the hands of many kids. Even so, the following questions remain: Are we seeing the results in student achievement that we should be expecting? Do these results justify the aforementioned spending?

A few years ago, the *Wall Street Journal* published a special insert on the impact of technology on education. The graphic on the front page depicted a student reaching as high as he could to use chalk on a blackboard. He was standing on a computer to reach higher—not a very flattering image. The image strongly suggests that we are using technology as a stepladder to continue to teach the same way we have been for a long time.

Technology proponents (techno-enamored nerds like me) argue that the widespread application of technology can reform schools, level the playing field for disadvantaged students, provide disabled students with real opportunities for participating in the mainstream, and create new opportunities for educators to build communities of best practices. The list of potential positives is extensive and even transformational—anytime/anywhere learning for all at a reasonable cost. Some of us even imagine bridging the digital divide while it continues to grow deeper every day.

To date, there is very little test data to suggest that the promise of improved learning for all has been met. What has gone wrong? Is the technology too difficult to use? Is staff development missing? Is education boxed in by government regulations that limit the creative use of powerful machines? Is the structure of schools, prescribed by the Industrial Age, too rigid, too hierarchical? Are we missing the critical mass of investment? Or does it just take a long time to ramp things up? Perhaps the critics have been right all along, and there is much less real promise than many of us want to believe.

One seminal thinker, Shoshana Zuboff (1988), a professor at the Harvard Business School, offers a possible explanation for why technology has not transformed education. Years ago, when researching the impact of technology on business, she discovered that an organization could spend a great deal of money, train everyone, and correctly install the network without achieving any significant improvements. She notes that General Motors spent more money than any other private organization in the world on technology during the 1980s. The end result was a lowering in the quality of cars. Why didn't technology make a difference?

Through her research, Zuboff (1988) observed that there were two very different approaches to the use of technology—automating and informating. Automating led to incremental improvements, while informating led to transformational improvements.

AUTOMATING

Automating is the more obvious and common approach to applying technology. *Automating* essentially means *"bolting" technology on top of current processes and procedures.* When an organization automates, the work remains the same, the locus of control remains the same, the time and place remain the same, and the relationships remain the same. The same processes solve the same problems. Automating can lead to incremental improvement, but in some cases, as with General Motors, the quality of work actually declines.

In schools, we have automated the report card, the card catalog, the pencil, various science lab instruments, and many other traditional assignments. Many schools have entire programs to automate the blackboard with PowerPoint presentations across the curriculum. We now use computers to print report cards faster, to look up library books faster, to edit the five-paragraph essay faster, and to collect data faster. Each can be an underutilization of the power of the technology. We do it because the work is familiar.

As Zuboff (1988) discovered time and again, faster does not necessarily mean better. For example, a high school librarian once asked me to review the term papers students had written before and after the card catalog was automated. She was concerned that the new and expensive automated system was lowering the rigor of student work. As I scanned student papers, I could not tell the difference, but she could. She pointed out a pattern in the authors referenced in each bibliography. Students who used the automated catalog had primarily selected books appearing in the top half of the alphabet. Students who had used the traditional card catalog had chosen books that spanned the entire alphabet. The ease of accessing the information via the online catalog had lowered the quality of student research. The librarian was no longer naively touting the power of the automated card catalog. This serves as a reminder to beware of unintended consequences when technology is introduced; they almost always exist.

INFORMATING

Zuboff (1988) observed that *informating* is a more powerful way of thinking about technology than automating. While informating can lead to a much higher quality improvement, it is much more difficult to implement. It is not that the technology is more difficult to learn; in fact, very often an informated application uses the same technology as an automated one. What makes informating more powerful is a shift of control and empowerment. The organization fundamentally changes the flow and control of information. With informating, people who previously did not have access to information or the responsibility to apply the information to solve problems find themselves more empowered. New technologies can leverage empowerment through access to new sources of information and relationships.

In an informated environment, more people have timely access to information. For example, parents and students have access to grades every day instead of once a quarter. Students have access to content information that was previously only available in the teacher's edition of the textbook or in a university. Teachers have access to knowledge about brain research and new technologies that was only available in staff-development workshops. With timely access to information comes the potential for a shift in responsibility. As many traditional companies and universities have already discovered the hard way, when the customer or the worker gains access to new sources of information, chaos and even disaster can rule. But the upside gain can result in a transformation of quality and new services.

It is unlikely that technology will improve learning without a powerful vision and without thoughtful and creative teachers challenging students to go beyond traditional expectations of achievement. Educators can certainly bolt technology on top of the current curriculum, and students can use the computer as a $1,000 pencil with which to write a five-paragraph essay for a grade. Or educators can challenge students to serve as co-authors with students in other countries to publish their work for a global audience.

As you read the stories in *Empowering Students With Technology*, you will see the beginning of a cultural shift toward collaboration and learning empowerment. Teachers are exploring new ways of collaborating with each other, the family, and the community to provide a much more supportive and challenging environment for students through a wider range of information-access and relationships.

MOVING TOWARD INFORMATING LEARNING

Perspective and leadership—not technology—are what distinguish automating from informating. When automating, the goal is to preserve the current structure. The essential question is, What technology can we buy and install to improve what we are currently doing? Informating revolves around a perspective of asking what new and timely information we can give people in the organization and what new relationships we can nurture to improve the quality. There is a fundamental shift of control with informating. Relationships change, schedules change, the use of space changes, and, most important, responsibility shifts to the person who is the closest to solving the problem. The same technology can be required for both informating and automating. What makes the difference is the flow and control of information and the change in the relationships. Automating reinforces the current relationship of control. Informating leads to empowerment.

In an automating model, the technology is the vision. In an informating model, technology is just the digital plumbing. It enables a fundamental change in the culture of learning where students assume much more responsibility for managing their own learning and where collegial and community relationships expand.

When automating, the main focus of planning is "Technology Planning." The essential questions are technocentric:

- What technology should we buy?
- Where should we put the technology?
- How do we train the teachers to use it?

Rather than allowing automating questions to guide planning, it is more important to examine what we should be flowing through the technology and the potential new relationships. When informating, the technology infrastructure is still essential, but it does not become the driving issue. Informating questions may include the following:

- What information do you need to improve your work?
- What new relationships can improve learning?
- What authentic relationships can you imagine for your students and educators?
- What technology do you want?

It is only natural for an organization to automate first. Automating preserves the organization's processes and structure. No one has to lose control of information, and new relationships are not required. Essentially, everything stays the same.

Informating requires thinking about opportunities that could not be achieved without the technology. Informating creates chaos and the potential for confusion of roles. It can be very messy from a management and leadership perspective. Some would argue that there is no compelling reason at this time for schools to informate. However, as online delivery of educational services and competition to the local school increases, there will be a very compelling reason to informate: competition.

Many creative, risk-taking educators are exploring informating opportunities right now. These teachers are linking students and, in some cases, their families, to new sources of information and new learning relationships. One of the most powerful lessons I have learned about student motivation is that if students are given an authentic audience, they work harder as a group than they work for their teacher alone. Creating authentic audiences for students is one of the emerging skills for teachers. Many teachers also agree that students generally work harder for an authentic audience than for a grade. Music and drama teachers explain that it is the audience in the auditorium that is the primary motivator of student practice. What if every teacher had a global auditorium to motivate students to do their best work? While the technology makes writing easier (automated), it can also provide access to new relationships for authentic assessment (informed). Ultimately, classrooms will become global communication centers and students will be connected to an increasing set of authentic relationships.

We should only expect to see incremental improvement when we bolt technology onto individual classrooms (automate) and keep the same assignments within the structure of the same teacher-student relationship we have had for the past eighty years. In other words, we can send students down to the computer lab to type a five-paragraph essay. The technology certainly makes it easier to edit and spell-check and add beautiful graphics to the text. By itself, this is automating, and we would not expect to see a transformational improvement in student writing. The unique opportunity the technology provides is that we can now publish that student's work for the world to see or we can connect that student directly to an authentic audience for review, such as with a retired veteran for an assignment on World War II.

It is possible to visit teachers who are teaching their students that there are very few limits to accessing information and people. The students in these classrooms understand technical skills, but they also understand something much more important: They are the first generation to be global publishers—to access the raw material of information and to create refined knowledge products for application. They understand the social skills of working with people who they will never meet face to face. They also understand that they need to take more responsibility for managing their own learning. They do not see the boundaries of school as a solid wall. They see school as a global communications center. Or as one New York City teacher explains, "My classroom is a place where you come and do work." It is incredibly exciting to watch students learn the skills they need while at the same time understanding that the work they are producing can potentially make a difference to other human beings.

In this stage of the transition from the isolated to the connected classroom, we need leaders who can help their colleagues understand how to move to a team-based environment. Teaching teachers to use technology is relatively simple (automating); helping teachers to share student work and to build relationships (informating) is a more complex opportunity (see Figure I.1). It is the difference between maintaining the relatively isolated classroom as its own entity and building a networked learning environment for students and a more professional culture for teachers. What this means is that the role of the superintendent and the principal to understand how to manage change becomes absolutely essential. Leaders do not need extensive technical skills. However, they do need to understand how to support risk-taking teachers and how to craft a vision where technology is clearly viewed as simply the digital plumbing.

Automate	*Informate*
Technology is bolted on top of standard operation procedure.	Technology is integrated.
Efficiency	Re-engineering
Same Information	• New information • More information • More accessible
Same culture, only the behavior changes	• Culture shifts • Value changes
Same organization	Learning organizations
Same schedule	• Schedule changes • Anytime
Same relationships	New and more relationships
Same locus of control	Permeable boundaries
Same policy	Flexible and adaptable policy

HOW TO USE THIS BOOK

Empowering Students With Technology contains anecdotes from the field of teaching that provide a glimpse into how to manage the transition of preparing students to work in the digital economy. Schools were originally designed with paper as the dominant medium. As my friend Gail Morse in Lizzard Lick, North Carolina would say, "We were paper trained." We are now hiring the last generation of teachers who "speak digital with an accent." However, I have learned that it does not really matter what technology was available when one was growing up; teachers who know very little about technology can challenge their students to do amazing things when given access to powerful information and communications networks.

Throughout *Empowering Students With Technology*, there are a number of e-ventures, or educational adventures, that teachers can immediately apply to their own teaching or that can be modified to suit various needs and subject areas. Regardless of the content area or technology used, critical thinking and inquiry are brought to bear on the learning situation. In addition, each chapter has a reflection page so that the reader can pause to reflect on his or her own teaching practices or attitudes. You are also invited to promote positive change by sharing and reflecting on the challenge questions with others.

Chapter 1: Teaching and Learning the Structure of Information

Rather than talk about making students computer literate or technically literate (I am guilty; I have written two computer literacy textbooks.), there are now two essential literacies: information literacy and communications literacy. Today's youth will grow up and work in a world that gives them access to massive amounts of information. Anyone can publish any version of the truth. The Internet is the wild, Wild West of information and there is no sheriff in town. It is essential that students learn information literacy: how to access and validate information and understand the organization of information. Communications literacy will also become a basic skill—if students do not understand the basic grammar of the Internet, they will be manipulated by people who do.

Chapter 2: Empowering Learning by Expanding Relationships

In a world with essentially free long-distance, videoconferencing, desktop, and handheld access to the Internet, today's students must learn how to work with people all over the world. The technical skills are easy. Teaching social interaction skills and teamwork skills is more difficult. Strategies and stories are shared in this chapter so that teachers can actively facilitate student interaction and global communication.

Chapter 3: Emerging Roles Within the Knowledge Community

Today's technology makes connecting with the community, finding resources, organizing data, and working on real problems much more manageable. It also necessitates change and new roles for the teacher and the learner. This chapter explores changing roles and how teacher leaders can grow with changes.

Chapter 4: Accessing Primary Sources to Enhance Critical Thinking

One of the most powerful uses of the Internet is to introduce students to primary source material. Rather than relying on textbooks to make meaning for students, teachers can now challenge students to construct their own knowledge.

Chapter 5: Online Learning

Online learning is becoming more popular as high schools and higher learning institutions add to their course offerings on the Internet daily. Pioneering efforts in online learning are discussed, and comments are included from parents, teachers, and administrators who have taken part in this phenomenon that is making learning opportunities available anywhere, anytime, and to anybody.

Ultimately, the introduction of technology to our schools is not about learning technical skills. Technical skills will become increasingly easier to learn. At the core of the change is a shift in the control of who manages learning. There are two essential questions to keep in mind when considering this idea: "How much control can students be given to manage their own learning?" and "What are the new collaboration opportunities for educators?"

Stay focused on what is flowing through the technology: information. Discipline your mind to make the technology invisible. The ideas, stories, skills, and exercises outlined in these chapters can provide you with strategies for empowering student success and helping bring students into the knowledge community.

Teaching and Learning the Structure of Information

INFORMATION LITERACY: A NEW BASIC SKILL

The impact of the Internet on students is already powerful, and it is growing every day. For many children, including my own, it is the dominant media of choice, replacing television or print. Now that students are choosing to use the Internet as their personal media, we are faced with the consequence of not teaching our children to decode the content. The growing persuasiveness of the Internet will lead to more and more students potentially being manipulated by the media. Too many young people believe that if they see it on the Internet, it must be true.

The Internet is a free and open global forum where anyone can express any version of the truth. It represents the most dangerous of information environments. As the Internet opens new worlds of access to art and music and research, it can be distracting and very seductive. Unfortunately, there are people and organizations that hope our schools do not teach students how to validate or evaluate the information they encounter on the Web. Understanding the grammar of the Internet, just as we do with print media, is the first step in helping students to be more astute and careful about how they interpret information on the World Wide Web. If you do not know the rules, it is impossible to win the game.

Zack's Story

Of all the stories I have collected about technology and learning, it was Zack's experience of finding a Web site published at Northwestern University that inspired me to write this book. That Web site, describing the Holocaust as an historic myth, is no longer available at the original address. In fact, when you type in the address, a screen from Northwestern appears that says the site is no longer available. The message is only accurate in part. The site is no longer available at the original address, but it is available if you know how to research the history of a Web site with a special tool called the *Wayback Machine*. In this revised edition of *Empowering Students With Technology*, I offer you the original, powerful story of how Zack came to believe the myth to be true and how you can find a site that is no longer available at its original address.

The Danger of Ignorance

A fourteen-year-old named Zack was asked what he was learning in school by his retired neighbor.

Zack answered, "I'm working on a history paper about how the Holocaust never happened."

The neighbor was incredulous. "Zack, where did you hear that the Holocaust didn't happen?"

> "I found it on the Internet in my high school library. Concentration camps were really clinics to help the Jews fight typhus carried by lice. . . ."
>
> Later that day, the neighbor called the school superintendent and demanded that the Internet be shut down.

This real experience of a student named Zack is a prime example of the way in which young minds can be manipulated if they are not educated in the necessary skills of validation and evaluation of Internet information.

How could a high school sophomore be fooled into thinking that death camps were really medical clinics? Zack was fooled because the Web site he relied on for his information belonged to a professor at Northwestern University, Arthur Butz. Professor Butz does not deny the existence of the camps. Instead, he explains the existence of the camps as an attempt by the German government to fight typhus carried by lice. He does not deny the shaving and the showers; the canisters of the gas, Zyklon; and the crematoria and the death. He calmly and simply explains these details as necessary actions for the eradication of pervasive lice. It is a persuasive document, and it has the domain name of "nwu.edu," which is Northwestern University.

Resources to Develop Critical Thinking Skills

- American Library Association
  http://www.ala.org/

- Mid-Continent Research for Education and Learning
  www.mcrel.org/

Think about this from the perspective of a fourteen-year-old who is untrained in thinking critically about information. He is researching the Holocaust, and by searching for the name of one of the chemicals used in the gas chambers, Zyklon, he finds a Web page of a professor at Northwestern University. His teacher told him to find a unique topic, and this certainly fits the bill. He has never heard these ideas before. The page is simple and clear. It is written in a calm, logical tone. From Zack's perspective, it is a valid source from a tenured professor at a top university. It has a 1990s publication date, and it is on the Internet. It must be "true." After all, Zack found his research from a Web page at http://pubweb.acns.nwu.edu/~abutz/index.html, titled Home Web Page of Arthur R. Butz.

The answers to the tough questions inherent in accessing the Internet lie in the ability and willingness of adults to teach students practical and usable methods for exploring the Internet, making meaning, and gaining a proper perspective on what they encounter there. With today's information explosion, it is essential that we teach our students to understand a range of strategies to cross-reference and to understand who controls the information they find. Too often, students use a search engine without the knowledge of how to question the information they find.

MAPPING THE INTERNET: META-WEB INFORMATION, AUTHOR, AND PURPOSE

While Zack did learn the technical skill of accessing the Internet with a search engine at school, he was not taught the critical thinking skills of understanding the structure of the information or how to cross-reference the source. His lack of knowledge of how to think critically about information made him a victim. Teaching students to use the Internet is much more complex than simply teaching them how to use a search engine to surf the Web. We need a comprehensive plan that teaches students how to access information and how to make meaning of what they access. One plan is MAPping—where students "map" the information they access on the Internet by examining

- **M**eta-web information
- **A**uthors
- **P**urpose

See Figure 1.1 for a brief summary of MAPping.

Meta-Web Information

It is a strongly held belief that teaching young children the structure of print information is essential: title of a book, author, table of contents, sentences, paragraphs, and index. With print, once you know the rules of the organization of information, you are more literate, and you are in a better position to interpret the information. There are rules, or grammar, that we can teach students so that they are in a better position to understand the context of the information on the Internet as well. It is impossible to use the rules of baseball to play a game of basketball and win. Similarly, if you take the grammar, or rules, of print to the Internet, you will not win. What we need to do is reveal the structure of information on the Internet to students. When we teach young people to read books, we teach them the grammar of print. This is also the logical starting point of teaching students to be literate with the Internet. There is an Internet grammar that necessitates that students know the Internet's equivalent to, among other things, footnotes, indexes, and bibliographies. And once it is understood, the medium becomes a much safer and more creative environment for both finding answers and publishing information.

The grammar of the Internet is contained in its meta-web information. *Meta* means *about*. Therefore, *meta-web information* refers to the workings and protocol of the Internet. By examining the meta-web information, students like Zack can put what they find on the Web into perspective. There are three parts to understanding meta-web information: web addresses, links, and search engines.

Figure 1.1 MAPping the Internet

Information on the Internet can be evaluated by mapping the following:

- Meta-web information—the structure of information on the Internet, including URLs, links, and search engines
- Author—anyone can post information on the Internet; credentials, such as professor or doctor, should not be accepted without evaluation
- Purpose—most sites sell products or services, advocate ideas, entertain, and/or present information

---

Understanding the Web Address

Basic Internet grammar begins with understanding the structure of the URL (universal resource locator), or address, of a Web page. Students need to be able to read the meaning of a Web address. Figure 1.2 dissects the Web address of the page that describes the use of Zyklon.

Can you read the structure of this Web address to decipher whether the professor's document is an official position of the university or a personal posting? There are two clues in the Web address that tell us that this page is *not* an official university document, but rather a posting in a personal directory. Every Web address, or URL, contains a home directory that includes the domain name of the organization. In this case, the first clue is embedded in the home directory "http://pubweb.acns.nwu.edu." *PubWeb* is a common term in Web addresses. It refers to a public Web server. Typically, a PubWeb is a machine on a network that is set aside as a depository of personal files. This should have been the first indicator to Zack that the posting he read was not an official university document.

The rest of the home directory tells us that the name of the PubWeb is "acns." Network administrators name file servers, and they can use any name they wish. The name ACNS has no grammatical meaning. What does have meaning is the "nwu.edu." Northwestern University owns the domain name nwu.edu. The *.edu* indicates that *nwu* is an organization of higher

Figure 1.2   Anatomy of a Web Address

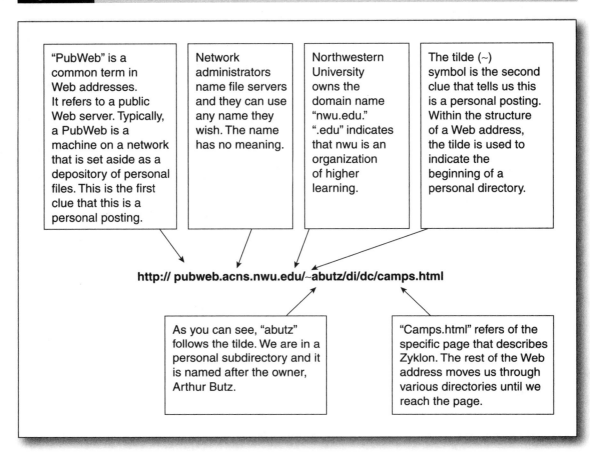

learning. If the domain name had ended with *.com*, it would not be a university; instead, it would be a commercial venture. Every year, the university must pay a fee to continue to reserve this name as a unique address on the Internet.

After the end of the home directory, the *.edu*, we see a forward slash (/) and then the tilde symbol (~) followed by "abutz." The tilde symbol is the second clue that tells us this is a personal posting. Within the structure of a Web address, the tilde followed by a name is used to indicate the beginning of a personal directory. Since "abutz" follows the tilde, we are in a personal subdirectory named after the owner, Arthur Butz. Then there are more forward slashes, and we move through two additional subdirectories, "/di" and "/dc." Finally, we are at the last bit of the address, "/camps.html." This refers to the specific page that describes Zyklon. The rest of the Web address moves us through various directories until we reach the page that describes the medical clinics. Unlike street addresses, Internet addresses begin with general information and end with the specific. There are no page numbers. It is the information that follows the last slash (camps.html) that is the reference to a specific page.

If Zack had been taught to read the general structure of URLs, he would see the "/~abutz" as an automatic giveaway that this is a personal Web site. Instead of misjudging the source as an official document published and endorsed by Northwestern University, Zack would know that it was equivalent to a bulletin board posted outside an office and did not have the gravitas of an official university document. In fact, at the time, and until July 2006, it was Northwestern's policy to allow any professor to use the network as an open forum to express ideas as long as they were not expressed as an official position of the university. It was in July 2006 when university officials made the decision to terminate all PubWeb accounts. No indication was made that this was due, in any part, to Professor Butz's site.

If it were not for the Wayback Machine, the closing of this Web site could quickly end our story about Zack. After all, the site is gone, so nobody will get their hands on it again. The Wayback Machine, found at http://www .archive.org, is a fantastic example of why students must be careful about what information they post online. A lot of the information on the Web never really dies. For example, what a student posts now in high school could be the information that will keep him from getting his dream job in the future because more and more employers are doing Web-based background checks on potential employees. Let's examine this a bit more closely.

Go to http://www.archive.org, and in the center of the page, you will see a box titled *Wayback Machine.* In that box, type the web address of Professor Butz's site: http://pubweb.acns.nwu.edu/~abutz/index.html. You will be taken to a page with several dates listed. These are dates when the Web archived this site. Select a date, and you will see what his complete Web site looked like on that date. Try this with your school's Web site. As you move back in the listed dates, you may see several different versions of the school Web site. While this is a helpful tool, it's also fun to look at the progression of a site over time.

The following **E-VENTURE** challenges students to invent a domain name for an organization or company. For any of the **E-VENTURES** offered throughout this book, students should be encouraged to reflect upon the lesson and their experiences in cyberspace by maintaining an electronic or hard-copy journal. They should make an entry each time they go online and an entry each time a lesson they have previously experienced comes in handy in the future.

E-VENTURE: Invent a Domain Name

Purpose: to help students understand the meaning and significance of a domain name

(Continued)

(Continued)

Investigation I

Ask each student to think of a domain name that best advertises them to the world. Ask why they've chosen their particular name.

Have students research whether or not their domain names are available. Have them go to www.register.com or a similar site. They should search .net and .gov derivations of their domain name.

Discuss how a domain name affects a user's perception of what might be found on that site.

E-VENTURE: Looking Back in Time

Purpose: to help students understand that information on the Web can live on even after a Web site has closed

Investigation II

Research the history of a site at www.archive.org.

Provide students with your school's Web address and ask them to find the site with the Wayback Machine. Teach your students how to type a Web address into the Wayback Machine in order to research the history of a Web site. Explain that they would still find the history of the Web site even if the site no longer existed.

Discuss the importance of being careful about building content on a Web site. People who have research skills may be able to find content that was once on a Web site for years into the future. Also, mention that being able to track the history of a Web site that is still currently available can be a very useful activity for tracking how a Web site has developed over many years and how content has been altered and updated.

Digital Threads: The Structure of Linked Information

Knowledge of Web addresses can also be used to try to validate information by discovering the pattern of links that point to any Web page. These links do not appear on the Web site itself. They are the shadow threads that emanate from other Web sites from across the Internet. Because the Internet is an open forum, it is possible that a Web author does not even know who has linked in. In fact, when I visit schools, I often ask if teachers and administrators are aware of how many sites around the world are linked into the school or district. They most often answer, "I do not know." Ignorance is not bliss. The Web is filled with millions of connections between Web sites that have never notified the linked site. Links are constantly being generated and broken. Wouldn't you want to know if and why there were links coming in to your Web site from around the world? How is the information on your Web site being used? What is the context of the judgment that other people are making about your site? Who are the people who have chosen your site as a source? What are their motives? Are they using their site to distort the context of the information on your site? Questions like these are critical to understanding the impact of any Web site within the structure of all linked information.

Links are the digital threads that connect Web sites to one another and that make the World Wide Web a true web. One of the strengths (some would say weaknesses) of the Internet is that anyone has the ability to add a link from his or her Web site to another. It is important to teach students that there is no link police force. Within seconds, essentially anyone with a little bit of technical knowledge can create a link to point or connect to someone else's Web site. Once you understand the structure of links, you can cross-reference sources on the Internet and gain perspective about the value of a source.

Connecting the Dots: Domain Names

com: commercial or profit organization
org: nonprofit
net: network
gov: government agency
k12: schools

For example, if you looked at my site, www.novemberlearning.com, you would find only wonderful things to read about me and my work. If you really wanted to gain perspective about the importance of my work, you would want to find out who is linked to my site. In this way, you can learn how various organizations, from schools to universities to companies, reference my work within the context of their own site. Building a pattern of links coming into a site does not tell you if any given information is right or wrong, but it does allow you to gain perspective. If you have a Web site, you may want to do a link search on your own site.

The first time I realized the potential abuse of power found in placing links on a page was when a colleague, a physics teacher, related an experience she had with some of her top physics students. Her students were researching comets and had found what they thought was a legitimate astrophysics site. On the home page, there were links to NASA and the Harvard Observatory. At that time, neither my colleague nor I understood that a link does not indicate a legitimate relationship or official endorsement of the site. As my colleague walked past two of her students who were exploring a comet Web site, she asked them to print the page so that she could read it later. To her horror, she discovered that it had little to do with astrophysics. While the Hale Bop Comet was the central theme, the focus of the message was not about science. The site was maintained by the cult who believed in the Hale Bop Comet as the signal of the end of the world. The cult members had used the links in an attempt to provide instant legitimacy to their site to make it more popular—a strategy that worked with some of her students. There are two critical pattern questions students should learn to ask about links:

- What can we learn from the pattern of links embedded in a Web site?
- What can we learn from the pattern of links pointing to a Web site from outside of the site?

Internet Sleuth: The Link Command

Finding the links embedded in a site is relatively easy. Using a mouse, drag the cursor across a link on the page. This action reveals the Web address at the left bottom corner of the screen.

Let's go back to Professor Butz's site that we found using the Wayback Machine. If we examine the link provided to us, we will see an address something like http://web.archive.org/web/20030418061633/**http://pubweb.acns.nwu.edu/~abutz/index.html**. The first part of this address is the site's archived address, while the second part, the part I have in bold, is what the address of the site was on Northwestern's Web server.

Following the second part of the URLs as we move our cursor over each link will show us something very important. Most of the links on Professor Butz's site are internal links. Each link points to information on another page of his site. This trend continues as you click links and dig deeper into Professor Butz's site. You can quickly determine this by noticing that each link contains "/~abutz/." He is often the sole source for his own work. This pattern of internal links should raise a red flag.

Figure 1.3 Example of Using the Link Command

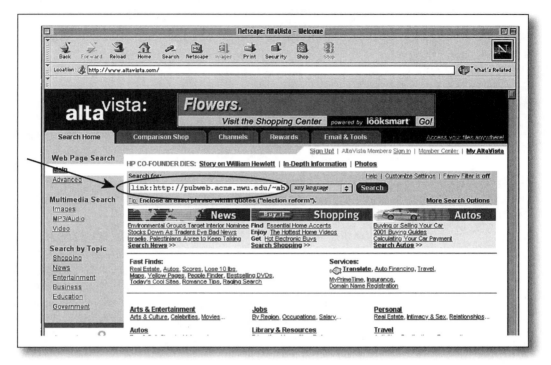

Figure 1.4 Steps for Using the Link Command

1. Copy the Web address of the source. Highlight the Web address by clicking in the location bar at the top of the Web browser, and then pull the edit menu down and release on the copy command. The Web address is now copied into the computer's memory.

2. Type www.altavista.com into the location bar and hit the return key. Now you are connected to Alta Vista. (Other search engines can also be used.)

3. Click in the empty rectangular search box and type the word *link:*. Do not forget the colon.

4. After the colon, paste the stored Web address by pulling down the edit menu and releasing on paste.

5. Click the search button.

6. Take a look at the listed results. You have created a list of sites that are linked into the original Web address.

Scanning the link addresses on a page is similar to reading footnotes. If every footnote of an article were by the author, would that raise a cautionary red flag for the potential of author bias? If every link on a Web page is a reference to another Web page by the same author, students should begin to question the potential of bias.

Finding the links pointing into a site requires knowledge of the structure of Web addresses and a search engine that provides the link command. While this search is more complex, it can provide a more revealing perspective than internal links. See Figure 1.3 and Figure 1.4 on page 21 for an example of using the link command and for the step-by-step process for using the link command.

Hints on Using the Link Command

Sometimes a link command will yield few or no related Web sites. In this case, truncate or shorten the Web address and use the more general section of the Web address for the cross-referencing.

By erasing the specific reference to one page (remember, this is the end of a Web address) and using the link command with a truncated Web address, you can search for any document that begins with the address of the personal directory.

Instead of searching for links that are directed at a specific page on the Web, truncating creates many more possible connections. In the example we are using, erase the specific reference to the document and the two subdirectories: "di/dc/camps.html."

Now copy the truncated version: http://pubweb.acns.nwu.edu/~abutz and use the link command at AltaVista to conduct another search for linked sites.

To begin his cross-referencing, Zack needs to know how to find all of the Web sites connected to the source at Northwestern. Who has taken the effort to link to Professor Butz? What does the pattern of these links reveal? The search engine AltaVista provides a free research service that gives a map of the links coming into any Web site. (Many other search engines, such as Google and Yahoo, can also reveal links related to a site.) Zack can use the link command to cross-reference Butz's page.

The list Zack could have created from the link command contains a wide range of Web sites for organizations such as university libraries and individuals, including me, who have chosen to create a link that points to http://pubweb.acns.nwu.edu/~abutz/di/dc/camps.html. Finding these links will not give Zack a definitive answer about the value of the information, but it will reveal how Butz's site fits into other sites. Zack will discover sites such as the White Nationalist Links at http://www.crusader.net/resources/links.html. Butz is on the same page as links to the Online Fascist Resource Page, Knights of Michigan KKK, White Power Central, and Texas Aryan Nationalist Skinheads. Sites that reveal that Professor Butz's views are not widely held include The Baltimore County Library. Arthur Butz is listed as a revisionist on their extensive Hate

Directory. My site can also be found with the link command because I have an article called "The Web: Teaching Zack to Think," which has a link to Arthur Butz as part of my efforts to explain why students need to be taught to think critically. In fact, the following is an e-mail I received from a student in Ohio who was directed to my site by his teacher and discovered the links within the context of my article.

Dear Sir:

I'm a high school student. Like Zack, I am doing a research paper about the Holocaust. Again, like Zack, I searched the Web. I came across an article about Zyklon B by Arthur R. Butz. It had the information I needed for the paper. That was last week. Just yesterday, my teacher showed me the article of yours, "The Web: Teaching Zack to Think." Now, I am questioning the credibility of Prof. Butz. I am now trying to find more information elsewhere. . . . Thank you again.

A High School Senior

In my two different searches, I found 58 sites linked to Butz's complete Web address for his most popular document, "A Short Introduction to the Study of Holocaust Revisionism," and 245 linked to the truncated link, the main page of his personal Web site. It is important for Zack to understand the structure of Web addresses if he is to become disciplined with his research strategies. When I used the link command, I found a teacher's Web site. This teacher challenges her students to look at four different Web sites, including those of Arthur Butz and the United States Holocaust Memorial Museum (http://www.ushmm.org/museum/exhibit/online/phistories/). This teacher is purposely introducing her students to Arthur Butz within the context of different points of view to see if her students can discriminate between versions of the truth. Juxtaposing different versions of the truth and challenging students to think critically can be a powerful teaching strategy.

E-VENTURE: Register.com

Purpose: to help students see how URLs are registered and who owns their favorite Web sites

Investigation

Led by the teacher, the class brainstorms 8 to 10 Web sites that they have visited and enjoyed either at home or at school. (Sites inappropriate to class

(Continued)

(Continued)

investigation because of a violent or otherwise unacceptable nature should not be used in this activity.)

1. The teacher writes each usable URL on a separate card.

2. The teacher forms the class into teams of three or four.

3. Each team draws a card.

4. Each team visits the site on the card, prints out its home page, and writes a brief description of the site that includes the following:

   • The site's author(s)
   • The site's apparent purpose

5. Using www.register.com, students research which company owns the URL.

6. Each team pastes the home page in the middle of a large piece of poster board with its URL written clearly above the printout. The company who owns the URL should be written below.

Presentation

Each team gives an oral presentation to the class using their visual, which explains which company owns their URL, why the company would have an interest in the Web site, and what those connections tell us about the site.

Variation

Using www.register.com, students may see how many variations of their URL exist. Then they can invent a new one.

Students may do further research about the company from their team's search. Students may research the company to see what other Web sites they own.

Questioning the credibility of sources that have every appearance of being credible will become an increasingly important skill. While anyone can publish information on the Web, the ability to instantly create a list of linked sites provides an information map that can give additional perspective to the original source. Once Zack understands the structure of the Web and how to map links, he can use this knowledge to question the validity of what initially appeared to be a very credible source.

Search Engines

Zack found Butz's page using a search engine and by entering "Zyklon" in his search. If Zack ran a search for "Arthur Butz," he might come across a page like the one at http://www.stormfront.org/forum/ showthread.php?t=92404, where Professor Butz is referred to as a "prominent historian" and his views are praised by members of the community at stormfront.org, a Web site dedicated to white supremacy. Coincidentally, the Stormfront group also owns martinlutherking.org, a site that claims to teach the "truth" about Martin Luther King, Jr.

Zack did not realize that search engine results also require evaluation. Search engines search databases of several different Internet directories to give the user results that are not always sorted the same way. For example, the search engine Google, at http://www.google.com, reports their results by overall popularity, while Answers.com's results pull from reference materials and Ask.com's results are ranked by experts in a particular field. Other search engines may list results by the number of times keywords appear in sites. With this in mind, just because a certain site is listed first does not mean it is the best or that it provides accurate information.

Zack did not know anything about Butz, but he could have researched his background. By using the search engine Ask.com, Zach would quickly see the swirling debate around this professor's work and would be able to make a better decision about using his material for scholarly purposes. The following **E-VENTURE** allows students to see the different ways search engines report search results.

E-VENTURE: Sorting Out Search Engines

Purpose: to guide students to see that the order of a search engine's results does not necessarily equate with the site's importance or accuracy

Investigation

1. Divide the class into four groups and assign each group to use a different search engine, such as Ask.com, Answers.com, AltaVista.com, or Google.com.

2. Choose a class research topic—a current news event, historical event, popular culture, or content area fact.

Presentation

Ask each group to report what they found to be the top five Web sites for each search for their one search engine.

Discuss how important it is to question how search results are ranked and how they are presented.

> ### Search Engines
>
> - http://www.Altavista.com
> - http://www.Answers.com
> - http://www.Infoseek.com
> - http://www.Yahoo.com
> - http://www.Ask.com
> - http://www.Noodletools.com
> - http://www.Google.com
> - http://www.Hotbot.com

Author

The second step in the MAPping process of validation involves the site's author. We all know that it is easy to fool people. Many people, especially children, will believe someone if he or she sounds authoritative. When I have talked to adults about Butz's Web site, they never fail to point out that, "Butz is a professor, sure, but he's an engineering professor, so he really does not have credibility as an historian. What really qualifies him to speak as an expert on the Holocaust?" Unfortunately too many students see *professor* and take what he says as official. Since anyone can publish information on the Internet, it is very important to investigate an author's credentials.

Purpose: Advocacy and Objectivity

The third step in the MAPping process is evaluating the site's purpose. When viewing a Web site, students need to learn the difference between advocacy and objectivity. During class discussions, we can teach students to ask fundamental questions about any site. We should always try to ascertain a Web site's purpose. Students should ask what the site is trying to do and why the site was created. Most Web sites are designed to sell services and products, to present information, to advocate ideas, or to entertain. Many sites do several of these at once.

A Web site's purpose is always clear. Look at Butz's site. His purpose is surely advocacy, although he comes across as an objective information provider—especially in the closing sentence of his article where he explains that thoughtful people should be skeptical of the death camp concept. Would that ring any warning bells for a fourteen-year-old? Are ninth-graders taught how to distinguish between objectivity and advocacy? Make sure that students understand the purpose of a Web site and that the purpose may not be entirely obvious.

CONFUSING TECHNICAL MASTERY WITH CRITICAL THINKING

Zack was fully equipped with all the technical expertise necessary to access the Internet, but his school failed to provide him with the tools to make sense of the information. The Internet is a place where you can find proof of essentially any belief system that you can imagine. It is a powerful and potentially manipulative environment.

Many young people can be deluded by a false sense of confidence when they think they know what they are doing. Students and adults alike too often mistake technical mastery with critical thinking. Increasingly, students will become victims of the expansive dark side of the Internet unless we teach the critical thinking skills necessary to make meaning out of the overwhelming and potentially manipulative amount of information that is now available and growing every day. Interesting Internet sites that focus on developing critical thinking skills include the American Library Association at http://www.ala.org and the Mid-Continent Regional Educational Laboratory at www.mcrel.org/. The following *E-VENTURE* is a way for students to apply critical thinking to material they encounter on the Internet.

E-VENTURE: Comparing for Understanding

Purpose: to compare two or three Web sites to determine their reliability, usability, and validity

Investigation

In advance of a class meeting, the teacher investigates two or three Web sites on the same topic or theme related to the content and curriculum under study. For example, a search of global warming sites might yield the following sites among thousands of others:

- EPA Global Warming Site
  http://www.epa.gov/climatechange

- Global Warming International Center
  http://www.globalwarming.net

- Global Warming Information Page
  http://www.globalwarming.org

(Continued)

(Continued)

In class, explain to students what can be understood about the sites just by reading parts of their respective URLs.

Ask the class to brainstorm evaluation criteria. Web sites dealing with the topic of evaluation can be visited prior to discussion. Consider some of the resources listed at http://library.usm.maine.edu/research/researchguides/webeval.php.

Presentation

Each student group ranks the usefulness of each site according to the criteria they established and reports their findings back to the class.

Variation

The students may make this one of many entries in their individual ongoing electronic bibliographies on any number of topics.

The final bibliography can be evaluated by classmates, students from other classes or schools, or visitors to a Web site on which it may be posted.

BLOCKING VERSUS ACCESS

None of these various research techniques provide a definitive answer about Arthur Butz, but they do provide many points of view. With a thoughtful teacher leading the discussion and requiring students to learn to question credibility, we can better prepare students to enter a world where they will have access to essentially any version of the truth. In the end, Zack's high school arranged for him to have an interview with a Jewish woman who lived in Europe during World War II. It is always a good idea to look beyond the Internet for sources of authentic information.

We should all be concerned about student access. The Internet can be a dangerous and manipulative environment. Policymakers and school leaders are perplexed by the challenge of balancing blocking and access. Are we protecting students too much by blocking? Are we exposing them too much by giving them personal responsibility for appropriate behavior while they are on the network? Both positions can be based on a naïve understanding of what students need to know.

I think it is safe to assume that in the future, our current elementary students will have twenty-four-hours-a-day, seven-days-a-week access to the Internet from a small, very fast, inexpensive "toy" they carry in their pocket. I cannot assume that we will be able to block the Internet as children access it from the playground. Blocking students from the Internet in school can be a short-term victory—a classic case of winning the battle and losing the war. Filtering without teaching students critical thinking skills is too often the swiftest and politically expedient thing to do.

Web Safety Sites

- Federal Bureau of Investigation
  http://www.fbi.gov/fbikids.htm

- Wired Safety
  http://www.wiredsafety.org

- Safe Kids
  http://www.safekids.com

The Digital Gutter

Today, too many policies are being instituted that attempt to solve the problem of inappropriate access by filtering. I have often found Arthur Butz's Web site on the networks of many schools that use these filters. Filtering can give students and teachers a false sense of security and safety. While teachers may be able to protect children in school, what happens to students when they leave school to go home at night or to a friend's house or the town library? Who is protecting them when they are not in school? Are parents taking the responsibility for teaching their children about ethical use?

During a videoconference at Stanford University, I had the opportunity to ask a survivor of three Holocaust concentration camps what he would advise educators to do. I asked him, "Should we purposely introduce our students to this kind of version of the truth?" He did not hesitate with his response: "Hitler would have prevented any such dialogue. We must teach our students how to discriminate between evidence and interpretation."

Children tend to be very trusting and naïve about the messages and underlying structures that have every potential of manipulating them. In addition to concerns about safety, policies should be based on knowledge about how to use the Internet, its structure, and how to deconstruct its layers. We must teach students to understand the rules of the game, or they will surely lose.

PROFESSIONAL GROWTH OPPORTUNITY

Relate and Reflect on Chapter 1

The following questions are intended to further promote discussion about learning in planning boards, department meetings, school board meetings, and inservice preparation. They do not require any technological skill or expertise to answer. Space is provided after each question so that you may begin to answer them here. Remember that there is no right or wrong answer.

- Can we define what it means to be information literate?

- Can we teach our students to have the skills essential to information literacy?

- Can we truly prepare students to be effective users of the most powerful medium?

Empowering Learning by Expanding Relationships

PLANNING FOR LEARNING (INSTEAD OF TECHNOLOGY)

Stop! No more misguided technology planning! We need to focus much less on teaching students to be computer literate and much more on teaching students to be information literate and communications literate. In this chapter, we will focus on expanding the boundaries of learning beyond the classroom. There is enormous opportunity to motivate and deepen our students understanding of complex issues by connecting them to authentic audiences around the world. We have powerful and easy-to-use tools. What is needed is a vision that will support a more authentic experience for our students and a realization that many of our students want to tap the social communication side of the Internet.

Our students have access to more technology than students anywhere in the world: home computers, cell phones, gaming machines, plasma televisions. . . . The real problem is not teaching technology skills. Many of our students can learn about technology as fast as—if not faster than—adults. What our students cannot learn on their own, and what makes teachers more important than ever, is the urgent need to teach critical thinking and global communications skills.

Imagine that technology will increasingly become smaller and smaller and easier and easier to use. As this happens, our students' access to information and communications will become more ubiquitous. Now is the time to focus on the essential skills that are beyond the technical. For example, our students do not need our permission to generate a free Web site or a blog. What they do need is to understand the ethics and social responsibility of managing a global voice. Too many school policies begin and end with blocking sites where students have access to free services, such as instant messenger, and blogging sites, such as Facebook or MySpace. We need to recognize that we cannot control what our students choose to do when they are not in school. They are voting to build content on the Web by the millions. This is a major teachable moment. We must overcome our initial response of blocking access with a higher-order set of skills that teach our students to use powerful communications tools to have a responsible global voice.

Our students will need to function well in a globally connected economy. Managing massive amounts of information and learning how to work with people all over the world will become the new basic skills.

Connecting to the Internet and producing content to put on the Web has become progressively easier—a matter of simply using your Internet-ready cell phone. What you do with the information you access is the critical skill. Communication skills will also become more important. The abilities to learn over the Internet and to work with people all over the world are already necessary skills in the knowledge society.

Currently, there is too much focus on the wrong types of technology planning. Measuring success by how many computers we have per student or how many classrooms are connected to the Internet is relatively meaningless. Planning is essential, but if we are asking the wrong questions, it will only be a waste of invaluable time, money, and resources. Compare technology planning to information communication planning. With technology planning, the techno-centric issues lead the discussion. For example:

- What technology should we buy to improve learning?
- How many computers?
- How many printers?
- How many Web cams?

These questions are like asking, "Should we buy three-holed paper, lined paper, blank 8.5 inch by 11 inch paper, or legal pads? Number two pencils or ballpoint pens?" Whether it is paper or megahertz, it is all just stuff. Many educators, as well as most people in any nontechnical business, do not know a lot of the details about what is inside a computer. And that is just fine. As with assignments on paper, what educators should be concerned about is the quality of the information and communication that is going in or coming out of the computer or cell phone or interactive white board. Of course we need to build the infrastructure and connect students to the Internet, but the vision of why we are installing very expensive equipment should be clear, and it should lead to important learning results. See the box for questions to ask when planning.

Critical Planning Questions

- Does technology really make a difference?
- Does the allocation of resources align with the primary objectives of the school?
- Do we have the capacity to support teachers after the technology is installed?
- Do we need to help each student's family understand our investment?
- Will we use technology to improve what we have always done (automate)?
- Can we use technology to do things for our students that we have never been able to do (informate)?
- Are there new basic skills that all of our students and teachers must have to meet the skill requirements of our society (Internet grammar)?

While it may seem as if there is an overwhelming amount of new communications technology and we have just begun to figure out what to do with one computer in the classroom, we are only at the early stages of technological development and connectivity. Gradually, more and more schools are moving toward 1 to 1 programs, where each student has his or her own laptop or other hand-held device; as improbable as it sounds, we are only a few years away from every student having his or her own wireless digital assistant. The size of a small paperback, it will contain the equivalent of every textbook we now hand out, include a built-in video camera, and connect to the Internet at speeds that allow students to download and broadcast video. The planning challenge is to imagine doing things that we have never been able to do in education, not simply improving upon what we are doing today. The real work for our educators is not learning one new technology after another, but redesigning the assignments we give students to be more rigorous and motivating and, when possible, more global. It is a more complex task than adding technology to our current set of assignments. Very likely, it represents a decade of work.

Creating Collaborative Partnerships

We can start teaching students how to utilize communication technologies effectively from the early primary grades through high school and beyond to create partnerships between students within their city, their country, or even around the world. In the first edition of this book, I wrote about how something as simple as a fax machine can provide young students with the opportunity to exchange content with others. Today, an Internet-ready kindergarten or 12th-grade AP History classroom can connect to other students for free around the world via a program such as Skype. We now live in a time of free global communications. It is time to tap this power to challenge our students to understand global collaboration.

Skype, which can be freely downloaded from http://www.skype.com, will allow anyone with a computer and an Internet connection to connect with anyone else around the world who has Skype installed on his or her end. Once connections are made, discussions can take place with people anywhere through both text chats and voice chats. On top of this, students can also exchange digital files they have created directly through Skype. The newest version of Skype even allows users to videoconference if both parties have a Web camera.

One of the most basic, yet most exciting uses of Skype I have witnessed occurred one day as I was visiting with a kindergarten class. The students in this class had invited their grandparents to take part in the day's activities. Students and grandparents were scattered around the room working on various projects. Unfortunately one student had no grandparent there and was really upset about it. As it turned out, this student's grandmother lived in India, and after some discussion, we learned that this child had been keeping in touch with her grandmother through short e-mail messages that were sent back and forth. Seeing an opportunity to help this one child and to broaden the experiences of the classroom, we sent an e-mail to this grandmother with directions for installing Skype. Before the end of the school day, the computer in the classroom started ringing and we instantly had a new guest in the classroom. I guarantee that you have never seen a more excited group of kids. Instantly, the room was buzzing with questions about how other students could talk to their grandparents on the computer too.

How to Create a Collaborative Partnership

Any two teachers can create a collaborative partnership by doing the following:

- Assigning pairs of buddies
- Brainstorming fun activities (For primary students, this might involve drawing activities, such as self-portraits, or a favorite meal. For older students, this might involve exchanging poetry, creating collaborative research projects, or having students take part in a debate. All of these items can be exchanged using Skype.)
- As projects progress, planning to have the two classes meet, if possible
- Talking to students about what it is like to meet someone via Skype first and then meet face-to-face. Discuss how it might be different if the buddies met face-to-face first

---

Skype in the Classroom

There are many ways to use Skype, or any free voice/video connection, within educational settings, and with the ease of installation, the technology itself can truly become secondary to the information it can bring us. Let us take a moment to look at a few real applications.

Group Work on a Project

Skype supports multiple people within a chat. Therefore, several students could get on Skype with students from their classes, as well as global partners, to work together on a collaborative project. While time zones will have an effect on this type of exchange, you will find that students can be quite creative in figuring out this dilemma. For elementary school students in London, for example, imagine the many discussions about health and nutrition that could come from doing something as simple as comparing their grocery lists to the grocery lists of students in Bangladesh. With Skype, this is possible.

Ask an Expert

In Falmouth, Massachusettes, students and teachers are working with researchers from the Woods Hole Oceanographic Institution (WHOI) on an important problem affecting our planet: global climate change. Students are experimenting and collecting research data while collaborating with researchers from WHOI. One method they use to keep in constant contact with these researchers is Skype. Skype allows students to contact their professional research partners to report data and ask questions about their experiments. One of the experts, Max Holmes, even helped teachers make connections with students doing similar research in Siberia!

Getting Help After Hours

We've all had the experience of students coming to us with incomplete homework that was not finished due to a lack of understanding. To combat this, a teacher might consider setting up virtual office hours for a bit of time each evening. Students would know that during that time each night, they could get on Skype and make contact with their teacher to ask questions.

Inclusion

Brian Crosby, a fourth-grade teacher at Agnes Risley School in Sparks, Nevada, was informed that he was to have a student who was being treated for leukemia as a part of his class. Unfortunately, due to the nature of the illness, the chances were good that he would never see this student, Celeste, in his class. With the help of community members who purchased a computer and Internet connection for Celeste, Mr. Crosby was able to set up Skype for her so that she could take part in class activities, through video, during a part of each school day.

REVISITING THE ROLE OF THE FAMILY

Currently, only a few schools have begun to experiment with the power of leveraging communications technology to engage the family directly in the learning process. In the long run, partnering with the home may be one of the most powerful uses of the Internet, especially in traditionally underserved communities. What do you think the typical response from a student is when a parent asks, "What did you learn in school today?" My own child's response is "Noth'n, Dad." My children are not the most comprehensive or accurate source of what happens in school, and they are not alone. This lack of accurate information does not breathe life into the parent-school connection. Imagine, instead, a very different parent-child conversation, one where the parent is not at the mercy of what information his or her own child will provide!

School-to-Family Connections

Of course, it is common sense and research supported that we should involve parents in their children's schoolwork. To date, it has been impractical to have parents present for classroom activities. Parent participation is often only limited to very special events, such as parent's night or the school play. The research about the importance of parent involvement as a support for student learning has been well documented for decades (Henderson & Berla, 1994). Yet traditional schooling does not provide enough opportunities to link students with their families in the midst of hectic everyday schedules. Imagine that teachers can increase parent involvement whenever the teachers believe that it will improve the work of a student or build the capacity in the home to improve learning. The Internet provides many opportunities for parents to validate the work of their children. The Internet can support parent involvement in real-time classroom projects from remote sites such as their workplace or the home. As bandwidth expands and costs drop, the boundaries between home and school will blur. Many of our students will be taught the teamwork skills of working with peers, teachers, and their parents. A parent who is able to join his or her child through videoconferencing while in school has a chance to become more involved in his or her child's education and to validate the importance of learning.

A trip to rural Iowa taught me to expand my view of how to value the role of parents as important partners for their children with videoconferencing. A fifth-grade teacher in Iowa introduced me to the powerful concept of videoconferencing. The teacher explained that he invited parents to access the class Web site and use the Web cam to watch and participate with their children as they presented book reports. Parents were asked to type in questions and comments about plot and character development. Imagine the difference in the conversations at home that evening when parents who had never before had a chance to participate with their child during a class activity were given that opportunity. Instead of the parent asking, "What did you do in school today?" there are high fives and a celebratory, "Weren't we great today?" or "How did your teacher and the class like the book report?" This opportunity gives teachers the chance to restore the critical role parents have historically played in educating their children.

Bridging the Digital Divide

Of course, every family does not have access to the Internet—the digital divide may represent the most important issue in our planning for educational technology. One of the most successful home-school equity projects is in Akron, Ohio, where teachers Karen Grindall and John Bennet have written grants that enable families to connect via cable modem to Portage Path school resources. Almost 90% of their student population receives free and reduced lunch. Since the project's inception, test scores on traditional measures have risen. When I attended an open house that celebrated the work, a parent explained how the project has changed long-held feelings, saying, "You know, many of us [parents] were school traumatized. We did not do well in school ourselves and it can be very difficult for us to feel comfortable on parent night or any event in school. The computer at home has changed those feelings. Now, it is much easier for me to get involved with my child's education and feel very positive about coming to school. The only problem is that my six-year-old thinks that I use the computer too much!" Tanesha, a fifth grader, offered her perspective: "I love having the computer at home because whatever I learn at school I can always go back and review in my living room. I think it helps me keep my goal of being on the honor roll each grading period. I don't think we could have afforded to have both the computer and Internet. I am really lucky to have this fun way to keep learning."

School-to-World Connections

The limits of the physical boundaries of classrooms will no longer prevent teachers from connecting students to the world. Judy Lee, in Texas City, Texas, is an early pioneer in broadcasting low-bandwidth, still video images from her classroom during a class duck-hatching project. One of the benefits of the Web cam is that Judy's students are more willing to respond to inquiries about the progress of the ducks' eggs from people from around the world than they are to her inquiries. Judy enjoys watching her students take the responsibility of researching answers for people they will never meet. Because ducks do not always hatch during school time, the video camera also extends the time/space boundaries of her classroom. Her students log on to track hatching progress with family members and friends after school and on weekends. Her classroom is actively engaging students in learning, even at times when the students are not in class.

Tips on setting up an effective videoconference are provided in Figure 2.1. More information on videoconferencing, as well as some fabulous examples of ways different institutions are using this resource to connect with others around the world, is available at http://en.wikipedia.org/wiki/Videoconferencing.

Figure 2.1	Elements of an Effective Videoconference

- Use an additional light source on the speaker or speakers. (Do not use fluorescent light.)
- Feature no more than three people in the video window at one time.
- Create cue cards to be held behind the camera to ensure "eye contact with audience, newscaster style."
- Speak loudly, distinctly, and slowly.
- Use props, photos, and/or short (two minutes or less) video clips to enhance your presentation.
- Allow for audience interaction at least every 10 minutes.
- Rehearse a presentation before going online with it.

(Adapted from The Global Schoolnet Foundation)

Cultural Connections

If you want to add authentic practice and motivation to a language class, connect the students to native speakers in another country. One of the funniest and most profound learning experiences that I have ever had is when I watched my colleague, Julia Gurrero, turn on the video camera in her sophomore honors Spanish class at Glenbrook North High School in Glenview, Illinois. A whiz at making connections throughout the Spanish-speaking world, Julia decided to connect her students to a class learning English in Puerto Rico. My job that day was to make sure the connections worked. For one male student, they worked too well. When our student met the female student in Puerto Rico, he began to stumble with his words. The young woman sensed that he was uncomfortable and asked him in perfect English if everything was OK. His response gave her an opportunity to poke fun at his cultural insensitivity.

PUERTO RICAN STUDENT: You seem hesitant. Is everything all right?

U.S. STUDENT: Well, you do not look like I thought you would look.

PUERTO RICAN STUDENT: (somewhat defiantly)   Oh yes? How do you think I should look?

| U.S. STUDENT: | Well you know. You should look more . . . Puerto |
| (sheepishly) | Rican. |

The U.S. student hesitated when he saw that the girl was blond-haired and blue-eyed. His limited understanding of the Hispanic culture combined with his reliance on stereotypes had biased his ability to accept the student's image on the screen. His language skills were fine. He just did not know how to apply them within the cultural context of Puerto Rico. The student did not have to review the video to know that he breached the etiquette of cultural sensitivity. His ignorance of what it means to look Puerto Rican was revealed by the live exchange with his peer. His classmates could not believe his lack of cultural awareness. There was immediate laughter from the Puerto Rican students (luckily, they had a sense of humor), and some of the U.S. students nearly fell off their chairs they were laughing so hard. The entire exchange was captured as a video file. After reviewing the video, his cultural misunderstanding was converted to a deep appreciation of not making hasty judgments about how someone in another country should look.

This is one of the advantages of real-time videoconferencing. Teachers can create more authentic applications of practicing a skill, such as communicating in a second language, and create opportunities for students to make more mistakes and to learn and remember. Embarrassing moments of cultural insensitivity can have a profound impact on memory! Every foreign language class should have access to real-time videoconferencing.

E-VENTURE: Information Campaign

Purpose: to see the differing perspectives on issues from a global perspective and to foster a value for other cultures and for people with different points of view

Investigation

1. The class brainstorms criteria for tracking a news story as covered by various news outlets.

2. Have each group devise a log sheet to chronicle data.

3. The teacher determines the duration of the project and how frequently a site, channel, or print resource should be monitored.

4. The teacher divides students into ten groups.

5. Each group is assigned to track a particular news story from one of the following sources:

Local newspaper	The *New York Times*
TASS News Agency	India News Agency
BBC News Online **http://bbc.co.uk**	All Africa.com **http://www.allafrica.com**

Presentation

Each group reports their findings weekly to the class. During the initial presentation, each group also tells the class about the news outlet they were monitoring: who runs it, the local politics of the originating country or region, the native language(s), and the audience.

The teacher coordinates the creation of a large grid or graph that visually depicts each group's data.

As the culminating project, each student determines what factors influenced the various outlets' coverage of the event and theorizes with research-based support why and how the way the news is covered influences the people who read the reports.

Variation

Turn the tables by having students track an election in a foreign country and analyze how it is reported and consequently viewed here.

Track news stories other than those pertaining to politics, such as natural disasters at home and abroad or scientific discoveries like the human genome project, AIDS research, or Mars exploration.

E-MAIL IN A CULTURAL CONTEXT

Adding communications capacity to a classroom can reveal how important it is to teach students to develop global communication skills and how far teachers have to go to prepare students to work in an interconnected global economy. Years ago, when I was the technology director at a Chicago-area high school, I suggested to a colleague who taught world history that instead of involving his students in a simulation of the Middle East conflict, where different classes would assume the role of different countries in a mock United Nations scenario, he could use the Internet to have his students communicate directly with people in the Middle East. When he realized he could really do this, he became very excited. I offered to teach his students the technical research skills. His students came down to my office in the library and asked me to help them send a message to a school in Israel. Their question for an Israeli was, "Will there be peace?" They were not prepared when the Israeli responded, "Peace depends on water rights."

They did not want their question confused with an answer that was not a direct response. The students instructed me to find another school that might answer their question. I refused. I suggested continuing the dialogue to learn more. The students did not agree. These students had not been taught to try to understand a problem from a different cultural or geographic perspective. With Lake Michigan at our shoreline, we did not have a water problem in Chicago. Our students could not intuitively understand the relationship of water rights and seeking peace. We had not taught them to imagine that their questions might not be the most relevant. Technology brings us the authentic opportunity to teach our students to value the perspectives of peoples who have a very different cultural, geographic, historical, or economic point of view.

Adding global conferencing to the learning experience did not automatically create deeper understanding for these students. In this case, it created confusion and cultural dissonance. Once again, the technical skills were easy. It was the negotiating and communication skills that needed to be developed. As we connect our students to the world, we need to focus much more of our staff development on preparing teachers to help students manage relationships and learn cultural negotiation. The technical training is necessary but trivial compared to the critical thinking skills.

Making Connections

The Worldwide Classroom, at http://www.worldwide.edu/travel_planner/pen_ pals.html, and ePALS, at http://www.epals.com/, are free services that help facilitate intercultural exchanges. These services allow people to link with partners for pen-pal e-mails and project exchanges.

TEACHER-CREATED WEB SITES

As databases and other Web-based materials in various subjects become available on the Net, it will become increasingly important for teachers across the curriculum to use Internet resources to motivate and support student learning. Teachers can do this by starting a simple Web site with services like the one at http://www.thinkquest.org/en/, which provides teachers with free Web site space and online tools.

Another option that I highly recommend is the use of a blog as a class Web page. With a blog, creating a class Web page is much more than disseminating information to students and their families. Using a blog truly promotes an interactive learning experience. With a blog, teachers are able to create content for students to think about and respond to immediately or over a long period of time. Additionally, a blog creates a great place for teachers to post student work for review by an authentic, worldwide audience.

PUBLISHING STUDENT WORK ON THE WEB

The sports field and the high school auditorium are two venues where we traditionally give our students the opportunity to perform in front of their communities. But these activities include a limited number of students for a few days each year. Having a real audience to motivate students can be a very powerful and positive force. Ask any music teacher or football coach what would happen to student focus, motivation, and intensity if the audience were removed—no more performances and no more games in the stadium. Some of these educators will tell you that the effect of the audience or crowd is one of the strongest catalysts of student motivation.

The Web represents an audience extraordinaire. It is virtually limitless and allows for connections to Peace Corps volunteers in developing countries, to the local senior citizen's center, and millions of others in between. Teachers who have never had a chance to challenge their students to present their work for authentic review now have almost unlimited capacity. The impact on student motivation can be awesome. Knowing when to tap into this potential is the goal of creative teachers.

One of the most fulfilling ways to use communication technologies is to challenge students to publish their work on the Web. Creating the connections that enable students to seek validation by community members, peers, and the adult world will increasingly become important across the curriculum. As children grow up, they have a developmental need to know that they can make a difference and be productive in society. Using communications technology to add value to the world is one way to teach students that they can make a difference and that their work is important. Many at-risk students are desperately seeking acknowledgement for the contribution they can make to their communities. The Web, often the media of choice for students, is a natural means for bringing this about. We need to end the relative isolation of the classroom and connect our educators and students to the world. It is time to celebrate the teaching and learning that is taking place in our schools on a daily basis.

By publishing student work on the Web, teachers can affirm the importance of the students and their work. In some ways, it is "back to the future"—a return to the concept of the family farm, where children knew they had important chores to do and did not question that they were essential to the survival of the family and community. Teachers can restore an element of how important it is for students to know that their work is being celebrated by their families and their communities.

Many of today's students have access to active communication on the Web whether we teach them to use the medium or not. The technical skill is not that difficult. Twelve-year-olds can build Web sites on their home computer. Teachers can help students learn

- What to say
- How to say it
- When to say it
- How to respond to feedback from a global audience

Since students' technical ability can outstrip their communication skills and their sense of social responsibility, it is very important for teachers to model the appropriate use of the Web as a communications medium. As more and more teachers create their own Web sites, students will learn how important it is to publish knowledge.

As more students publish their work, teachers can take advantage of one of the most powerful pedagogies: showing students the work of other students in the same subject. One of the best resources on the Internet for this purpose is Thinkquest.org, at http://www.thinkquest.org/pls/html/think.library. This directory holds thousands of student projects, of which several are authored by international teams of students. Watch what happens when students preview what other students have accomplished in different parts of the world. Students have a natural tendency to want to improve the work of other students.

PROFESSIONAL GROWTH OPPORTUNITY

Relate and Reflect on Chapter 2

The following questions are intended to further promote discussion about learning in planning boards, department meetings, school board meetings, and inservice preparation and graduate courses. They do not require any technological skill or expertise to answer. Space is provided after each question so that you may begin to answer them here. Remember that there is no right or wrong answer.

- How can using technologies such as the fax, e-mail, the Internet, and real-time video create unique learning opportunities to help motivate students to excel?

- What are the new opportunities for family involvement?

- What would be the impact on teaching and learning if every parent had access to daily information about their children's progress at school?

- If every teacher had a Web site, what would be the most efficient design for teachers to share their best practices?

- Now that there is unlimited potential to celebrate the work of students with their communities, what is the best way to manage this opportunity?

- How can we create authentic work and relationships for our students to give them a deeper meaning in relation to complex issues such as globalization and cultural sensitivity?

Emerging Roles Within the Knowledge Community

TEACHERS AS DIGITAL IMMIGRANTS

In immigrant families, the children often learn the ways of the new culture—such as language, music, and slang—before the adults. It is not that the kids are smarter; it is just that they have less to give up. They are more willing and more motivated to learn because they want to fit in with their peers, with whom they are in constant contact at school. In many ways, teachers are like digital immigrants. They are not native born to this world of technology. Our students, especially our elementary students, are similar to second-generation immigrants. They have almost nothing to lose, and they see technology as an easy plaything, while adults might see it as a challenge. I have experienced what it is like to be an immigrant in my own land: school. Immigrants survive.

The real bottleneck to the creative use of technology is staff development. There are too many exciting technologies—Web design, digital video editing, presentation tools, probes, content specific tools—and not enough time for teachers to learn them. To be realistic about managing the transition from the isolated to the connected classroom, we may have to let go of our traditional strategies. At the top of my list of letting go is the idea that teachers must learn new skills before the students. It would be folly not to take advantage of how fast students can learn technical skills and how willing they are to be helpful—as the relationship between Yves, whose story was discussed in the Preface, and me illustrates well.

Following his break-in at the computer lab, I asked Yves to teach me what he knew about programming. I can remember feeling overwhelmed with what looked to me like a combination of mathematics and a foreign language, but it was not quite like any math I had ever seen! Fortunately, Yves was patient and enjoyed his role as the teacher. He made programming fun and accessible. He taught me how to develop strategies for testing my own progress. What I thought would be laborious and boring turned into a learning adventure. I could really tame the machine! It was the beginning of what would be many role changes from the traditional teacher-student relationship for me. I was a student again. My student was my teacher.

Reverse Mentoring

Teachers do not need a lot of technical skills. Teachers need an ability to manage the use of many technologies in the classroom without having to know the technical details. Managing student brainpower is one of the most important survival skills for teachers. For example, requiring or expecting every teacher to learn how to design his or her own Web site is impractical today. But asking students in the class to learn how to design a Web site is feasible, fast, and inexpensive. How many fifth graders do you think will raise their hands when their teacher asks for help with building a world-class Web site? Teachers should maintain the role of publisher and editor in chief of the material on the class Web site. The essential skill is to know what to publish, when to publish, and how to help students make meaning of the feedback from people around the world. Of course, asking students for help is a skill that some teachers will have to polish or learn from scratch.

Building a Class Web Site

The teacher should act as publisher and editor in chief.
   The teacher should practice reverse mentoring.
   The essential skills to know include

- What to publish
- When to publish
- How to help students make meaning of feedback

The teacher should allow students to manage their own learning—up to a point.

To put reverse mentoring into practice, find two or three students who can serve as your mentors. Ask your students to teach you what they have been doing on the Internet, especially from home. If students have a favorite digital skill, such as video editing, Web design, or working in Adobe Photoshop, ask them to give you an introductory lesson. Students often pick up skills outside of school that can add value to a teacher's understanding of the impact of technology on student motivation. Do not worry about actually learning the skill. It is more important to learn what students can do with the skill that might add value to their class work. For example, once you learn how easy it is for a student to do video editing, you might provide the student with the option of producing a video documentary instead of handing in a paper.

As more technology finds its way into the classroom, teachers are faced with the challenge and opportunity of giving up control of the traditional teaching/learning dynamic. I found that the more control I gave to the students to manage their own learning (up to a point), the more students excelled. Technology is not necessary for teachers to practice reverse mentoring, but it is a powerful catalyst for reshaping the prevailing dynamic with a dynamic that is better suited to today's environment.

HELP AND SUPPORT IN YOUR OWN BACKYARD

In the traditional classroom setting, teachers often find themselves isolated from their colleagues and the community during the school day. In many ways, teaching is a solitary job. While there is a tremendous amount of knowledge and wisdom within the profession, it can sometimes be very hard to access. Quite often, teachers in the same building are not aware of the unique skills and insights of one another.

The circumstances that have enforced this isolation are beginning to change because of the pressures and potential brought about by the digital world. Beyond school, the newly connected knowledge society increasingly requires a more flexible role for workers across many professions. Having knowledge is not enough anymore. Collaboration and sharing knowledge are the highly prized skills. This expectation of collaboration will eventually reach the teaching profession. Teachers will be valued for their ability to share their knowledge and solve problems about teaching and learning that an individual teacher could not solve alone. For example, as bandwidth increases and live video is installed, teachers will be able to share best practices as exemplified in their own classrooms with other educators.

Collegiality

As online learning explodes, more teachers build Web sites to support learning, and families gain more access to information about the progress of their children, collegiality will become more practical and necessary. Every teacher's best ideas can now be published so that other teachers and, in turn, their students, can benefit from them. If we expect students to be able to publish to a global audience, it is essential for teachers to model this same skill.

For reasons that once made sense, the organization of schools was designed in the mold of a highly controlled and departmentalized Industrial Age model. School organizations are filled with boundaries, such as departments and grades, that can impede the exchange of ideas and the development of innovation. The school leader's role is to make sure that these boundaries become permeable.

C. Edwards Deming, a leading proponent of the quality movement, taught that one of the very first things leaders can do to help colleagues adapt innovation is to honor them in their current paradigm (Rinehart, 1993). We need to honor the knowledge and wisdom of teachers. You will not find a more humble profession than teaching. It is time to celebrate the best practices of all teachers. Each school can use the Web to share the powerful stories that represent teachers' experiences. On a wonderful site by the Advanced Learning Technologies in Education Consortia, at www.4teachers.org, teachers can share ideas they have that work and find ideas for "powering learning with technology."

Additionally, in many school districts across the United States and around the world, teachers are being given access to laptop computers and hand-held devices for their use both at school and at home. This gives teachers a chance to share with colleagues their ideas that work—through e-mail, blogs, wikis, and videoconferencing.

The Anonymous Reviewer

One of the most powerful and helpful online collegial relationships is that of the anonymous distant reviewer. Kathie English and Nancy Hoatson, from Aurora High School in Nebraska, connected their students to editors across the Internet. They learned that expanding student relationships with distant anonymous reviewers can be a powerful motivator for students to improve their writing. English and Hoatson explain on www.4teachers.org:

> The [online] forum encourages students to produce more text and their reviewers to comment more honestly. Each piece of writing is considered for its own merit with no regard to author status: economic, social, or academic. Due to this anonymity, authors [students] cannot blame criticism on outside factors; therefore, they tend to heed the suggestions made by reviewers and, as a result, improve their writing. Reviewers enjoy the distance as well and tend to give more honest responses than they might in face-to-face peer editing.

While English and Hoatson found editors and writers to provide assessment services, any two teachers can create an assessment partnership. When a teacher assesses student work from another's classroom, there can be a very positive impact on student motivation and quality. The role of the face-to-face teacher can switch from judge to student advocate, helping students to understand how to interpret the outside review. When students no longer worry about personal judgments from their own teacher, students are more willing to make mistakes and to accept criticism.

In addition, the concept of teachers who share the review of student work has enormous implications for professional growth. If teachers are trading assessment services, the comments of each partner teacher are bound to add depth to the knowledge base of the team. Staff development becomes a normal part of the ongoing team relationship.

An international teaming of a teacher in England with a teacher in Japan illustrates how teachers can share knowledge as part of the ongoing process of sharing student assessment. In this case, a British teacher needed help with assessing her students' haiku. The teacher in England searched the Internet for a teacher in Japan who was also teaching haiku. When the assessment came back from Japan, the teacher in England was surprised and enlightened. "Haiku has a philosophy of life-giving forms," the Japanese teacher commented. "Imagery in the poem is very important and must be consistent with the philosophy. Some images that your students are using are not appropriate for the haiku form." The British teacher had been teaching haiku for many years in a very prestigious high school, but the exchange of student work allowed her to deepen her own understanding of the subject.

Collaboration With Parents

An obvious resource for teacher support is a parent or guardian. The role of the family in the learning process is well researched. One of the most powerful technologies to promote collaboration between the home and school is video. Many schools are utilizing video production as a means of sharing student work with parents at home. Contrary to popular thought, a video camera is a more developmentally appropriate device for a primary student to show expression and communicate than a pencil. Many parents will watch videos of their kids in the comfort of their own homes. It would not be unusual for tapes or DVDs to be shared with grandparents and be reviewed again and again. This technology can give teachers a powerful tool for sharing and celebrating student projects and providing parents with insights into how their students learn. In some cases, parents will send in videos of their comments. This media can add a level of communication and understanding that paper does not provide. The home VCR or DVD player and the color TV are "sleeper" technologies. They are readily available, easy to use, inexpensive, and possibly the fastest and easiest way to improve learning. It is just that there is very little tradition of building strong collaborations between the home and school.

E-VENTURE: Dino Documentary

Purpose: to allow for creativity, expression, and connection among and between students in the primary grades and beyond

Investigation

1. Using the Internet, interviews with experts, print materials, and observation during field trips, students create a simple script for a dino documentary.

2. Kindergartners, first graders, and second graders will need assistance from adults to construct the script, which should be written out on cue cards for nonreaders using a mix of symbols, pictures, and words.

3. Students film the project, or projects, using a digital video camera. Students should be able to function as cinematographers with supervision and appropriate respect for the value and function of the equipment.

Presentation

1. The film can be played at open houses or curriculum nights and can be made available on a JPEG file on the class, school, or district Web site.

2. Teachers can coordinate an online film festival where films are viewed and critiqued by students from other parts of the state or country, or from another country.

Variation

1. While this technology is easy for younger students to employ, it works equally well for older students. They can create their own documentaries related to stream monitoring or other ecological projects, homelessness, education, volunteerism, "a day in the life of . . .," or any other appropriate topic.

2. Students may adapt fiction books to film production.

3. Older students studying foreign languages can serve as translators for the primary grade film projects by writing subtitles for the films that will be shown to non-English language audiences.

4. Students may be asked to dramatize an original piece of fiction that one or all of them has created.

BENCHMARKING EDUCATIONAL PRACTICE TO THE KNOWLEDGE COMMUNITY

In a recent conversation with high school students, they expressed a clear desire that their teachers understand the world outside of school. Knowing this, teachers may want to consider reading about topics outside of education to track developments in the knowledge society. An indirect way to look into the world outside of education is to read material written for that audience. Magazines such as *Fast Company* and *Red Herring* are filled with stories of real people building the digital economy and the trends that are reshaping the structure of many organizations.

Business Technology Sources

- Fast Company
  www.fastcompany.com

- Red Herring
  www.redherring.com

Another way to benchmark against other industries that can be even more eye opening is to spend time with someone who works in a business that depends upon technology for its survival, such as banking, medicine, printing, or farming. Observing a friend or a parent of one of your students on the job gives you a direct link to information. See Figure 3.1 for a list of observation questions to ask during your visit.

Figure 3.1   On-the-Job Observation Questions

- What technologies are used?
- Could the business function without the technology?
- What sources of information are needed to manage the business?
- Does the business depend on the Web for any part of its work?
- How do people work together?
- How is the quality of work measured?
- What are the essential skills in the business?
- Does the technology create opportunities for new relationships, services, or markets?
- Are there skills that we could be teaching in school to prepare students for this kind of work?
- Are there leadership skills that can be adopted by the school organization to improve the quality of work?
- Are there any specific problems that students can try to solve?

SHIFTING CONTROL

Armed with new knowledge from my benchmarking, I designed a course that would not teach any programming—heresy at the time—and instead would focus on new tools and problem solving. On the first day of the new course, I boldly announced to my students that they would be the ones who would come up with the problems for the course. My role would be to teach them how to use the technical tools and to help them define and develop solutions for their problems. When I was finished with my introductory remarks, I cheerfully invited the students to share examples of problems in the world that they would like to solve. No one moved, no hand was raised; it was as if I had asked them to be absolutely silent and still. Finally, there was movement. A female student sitting in the front row explained the appropriate roles to me. "Mr. November, you are the teacher and we are the students. You are supposed to give us the problems. It does not work the other way around." There it was, simple and clearly stated: the definition of the high school teacher-student relationship in three sentences. The teacher teaches and then the students are taught.

My request was counter to the culture of schooling. In retrospect, it was naïve. While students must be given the opportunity to solve real problems that have meaning to them, they cannot be left adrift without guidance in how to define problems and how to progress. If schools have conditioned students to see teachers as people who assume control for managing learning, then it is unfair to expect students to take the initiative with problem solving. The responsibility for learning must shift to the students if we expect them to solve real problems in and out of the classroom. While it is a struggle to redefine and unteach the traditional roles for both the students and teachers, the process of shifting control of who owns the problems can result in some of the most motivated and focused student work possible. It just takes a while to get started and a willingness to shift control of who manages learning from the teacher to the students.

This shift in control was realized by Mrs. Taylor, a middle school social studies teacher in Deerfield, Illinois, who wanted her students to deeply understand the issues involved in globalization. In the past, her students would have read articles and written reports (some found with a search engine on the Internet) to get all of the information they needed and to relay what they had learned. This year, her students used Skype to contact a worker in Chicago who lost his job to outsourcing. She then arranged a live conversation with a worker in China who gained a job that was lost in the United States. Her students' understanding of the issues extended beyond the story portrayed in words. Her students were more engaged to frame the questions and to debrief the meaning of globalization in terms of what happens to real people on opposite sides of the planet. An added bonus of the project is that these conversations were recorded and published on the class blog. Students and teachers studying globalization in England listened to these conversations and benefited from the work of the students in Chicago.

By allowing students to work with global partners in this way, teachers can empower students by teaching them how to seek answers to their own questions. As students grow older, teachers can teach them to do high-quality research for real clients. At the same time, we can link these authentic experiences to make learning standards real and exciting.

Real Problems

The teacher's emerging role in a classroom centered on solving real problems is to facilitate student discovery, to offer resources, and to ask timely questions that refine and extend student thinking. The teacher needs to identify, with student input, an ill-structured problem, and then establish guideposts to help students address and define that problem. Technology in its various forms and degrees cannot solve a problem absent human input. Technology can provide a means for several functions (see Figure 3.2).

Figure 3.2	What Technology Can Do

Technology can provide a means for

- Simplifying calculation—calculators and spreadsheets
- Accessing information—the Internet and e-mail correspondence with experts
- Producing data logs—probes and personal digital assistants (PDAs)
- Displaying findings—presentation software and Web sites
- Making long-distance people-to-people connections—telephone, fax, e-mail, videoconferencing, voice over IP

When technological tools used in the real world are put in the hands of students, those students can better see themselves as problem solvers and can better and more fully communicate their capacity to solve problems to the larger world community. By giving students access to powerful machines, a wide range of problems that would ordinarily be beyond the reach of students to solve can become achievable. The number of student projects adding value to the world is extensive and growing, from extending the longevity of blood plasma supplies by a New York city biology student, to applying systems thinking and calculus to design shopping malls by a San Francisco student, to the digital recordings of American Indian chants of the Southwest by a Red Rock, Oklahoma student. Technology does not replace the importance of the teacher, but rather extends the teacher's role to challenge students to exceed their own expectations. One of the highest forms of validating the importance of teachers is to have students apply what is learned in class in order to add value to the world.

Real problems exist in every subject taught. Each year, find one real problem that your students can help solve. The people who will benefit from student action and investigation into the real problem can be called *clients*. One of the most important skills to teach students is how to conduct the initial client interview. Many students expect that the adult will know exactly what they want to see in a project. This is usually not the case. Students must be prepared to lead the client interview with a set of core questions for a discussion that can generate a clear understanding of the scope of the project with realistic expectations (see Figure 3.3). It may be helpful to invite potential clients to come in to class and to have students conduct their interviews there.

Figure 3.3	Questions for the Client Interview

- What is the current project or problem to be solved?
- Who is involved, and what are their roles?
- Who can help contribute to the solution?
- What information sources are available for the project?
- Has anyone else tried to solve this problem?
- Is there a desired format for the final project (database, Web site, presentation)?
- How will the project be evaluated for success?

Teachers can use parent conferences as a time to ask parents to offer real problems that are aligned with curriculum and state standards. For example, a parent who is a police officer provided sample police reports of real accidents to the Algebra 1 class. The students measured skid marks on the road and used algebraic equations to calculate the speed of the car. The class took raw data from an accident scene and wrote a police report and submitted it via e-mail to the lieutenant for review. How motivated do you think high school freshmen are when their assignment is going to be reviewed by the police department?

RAISING EXPECTATIONS: STUDENTS AS KNOWLEDGE PRODUCERS

While students have to learn to take responsibility for inventing and managing their own work, teachers need to raise their expectations of what students can accomplish. Emerging technologies can fundamentally challenge the current (low) expectations that exist for many students. For example, the power of probes or computer-based labs (CBLs) generates real-time feedback in the form of graphs as real events happen. This demonstrates that technology can help raise the level of what students can learn. Educators such as Carolyn Staudt at the Concord Consortium, at http://www.concord.org, now realize that we can teach middle school students to apply concepts from calculus to everyday life, fourth- and fifth-grade students to examine rates of change, and second-grade students to explore models of heat transfer using data loggers. One of the major barriers to using technology well is that many of the expectations for student success were set when the dominant media was paper and chalk. Paper is a very powerful medium, but it is not dynamic and it does not provide the sound, animation, real-time feedback, and capacity for continuous expansion of global relationships. Powerful machines allow for more dynamic teaching, and best of all, perhaps, they allow students to show what they know in nontraditional and nonlinear ways that more closely approximate the skills they will need to be successful in the adult world.

To illustrate, a student named Colleen taught me to expand my expectations of what young adults are willing to do in order to solve a real problem—especially if the solution adds value to the community. The clients are a social service agency and individual disabled persons.

Colleen's Story

Colleen's Health Care Database Project

By the time Colleen was enrolled in a course I was teaching, she was a veteran at avoiding schoolwork. In her, I saw a student slipping through the cracks. Somewhere along the line, I learned that someone in her family was physically disabled, and I knew that a local social service agency needed some help with organizing services for the community's disabled population. I invited one of the social workers to come to class to present that organization's real problem. The problem was providing the handicapped community with access to information. While there were a number of services available for the area's disabled population, potential clients' awareness of the services was limited. Sure enough, this problem touched Colleen and inspired her to work harder than she had ever worked before. With the guidance of a local agency, Colleen decided to create a database to list all of the recreational services available for the handicapped population in the greater Boston area.

Colleen's project grew so large that she had to enroll the volunteer help of her friends. Now there were students coming into the computer lab after school who were not taking the course, and they were willing to learn how to use a database to produce this knowledge product. The final project included the services of nearly 100 agencies in eastern Massachusetts.

Colleen deserved to be proud of her accomplishments. Ultimately, her work was recognized by a team of professional health care providers who asked if they could pay her to continue to expand her work. She was asked to train adults to expand her database. She refused to accept the payment. Her work was important to her, and she politely explained that this was her project and that she did not start it to earn money. She volunteered to come to school during that summer to continue her work. There is no way that I would have predicted at the beginning of the year that she would show that kind of personal commitment to solving a problem. I had to learn to recalibrate my understanding of student motivation. When the control of managing work shifts to the student, expectations need to be raised.

Colleen also taught me that students who are labeled as failures can have the integrity to define, manage, and persist at solving a complex problem—even when the design parameters are constantly shifting. Although Colleen never did well on the written tests that I gave in class, she had thrown herself into the practical and important work of creating a database. Through this experience, Colleen became a different person; she was motivated and actually glad to come to school.

Promoting Student Responsibility for Learning

As Colleen's story shows, it is important for students to share in identifying the problem. Students must have a sense of owning the problem rather than seeing it as an assignment from the teacher. Teachers can certainly help students shape a problem and identify resources and tools. Figure 3.4 shows how teachers can facilitate student acquisition of the skills necessary to deal with the rigors of real-world problems.

Figure 3.4 Skills to Solve Real Problems

Skill Needed	Teacher Facilitation
Communication	Role playing on video to allow for self- and peer-evaluation. Practice with written communication for inquiry and analysis.
Confidence	Access to feedback from outside reviewers (students, teachers, clients) to allow students to broaden their self-perceptions by seeing how their work is received by a potentially global audience.
Critical thinking	Teach students the grammar of the Internet and the critical thinking strategies necessary to evaluate information they encounter through their exploration and inquiry (see Chapter 1).
Interpreting data	Facilitate interactions and activities that allow students to collect their own data, evaluate, present, and draw conclusions from PDAs, probes, and large-scale student-conducted surveys.
Collaboration	Teach the project management skill of organizing and assigning work to different members of a team. Collaboration is an essential skill for our emerging

Figure 3.4 (Continued)

Skill Needed	Teacher Facilitation
	knowledge society. Big projects, such as Colleen's database, require many different skills, from graphic design to communications with clients to database programming.
Organization	Provide guidance with establishing realistic expectations of project management, including a clear description of the project, timelines, job descriptions, and communication between team members. New and evolving project management can help with this.

Drawing on areas of student interest promotes fully engaged learning, as Colleen's story demonstrates. She was passionate about issues related to people with disabilities because of her personal experience. Likewise, using media that students are interested in adds another compelling dimension. Video recording is a good example. It is amazing what students are able to do when given a video camera or a tape recorder and allowed to use these tools in their research. When students create a video of an environmental problem they are studying or record interviews with those affected by the problem, it can create great excitement in a project and add to the real-world skills they learn in the process.

Colleen's experience creating the database not only helped her become a better student, it also helped her contribute to society. Students, young and old, have an unlimited capacity to add value to their communities when given the opportunity. One of the most powerful uses of communications technologies is to connect students to real clients who have real problems to solve. In Madison, Wisconsin, and in St. Louis Park Schools in Minnesota, children in the fourth grade use the Internet to explore their communities and to compile research updates for their own state legislators. These students are doing more than taking part in the educational standard of learning how state government works. They are also directly participating as citizens in state government. Within Colleen's story is the blueprint for a learning environment that promotes student assumption of responsibility for learning (see Figure 3.5).

Figure 3.5 Promoting Responsibility

- Encourage and expect students to construct their own knowledge.
- Allow students to work with their preferred media.
- Choose real problems that are ill-structured with more than one answer.

- Have students add value to their community and the world.
- Ask students to develop a team approach.
- The teacher takes on the role of collaborator.
- Publish results of student inquiries.
- Link problem-solving skills to standards.

E-VENTURE: Connecting With Congress

Purpose: to facilitate student connections to the real world by allowing for access to real problems and avenues for addressing those problems

Investigation

Using the Thomas Legislative Information on http://thomas.loc.gov (a service of the Library of Congress), or simply by reading the newspaper, the teacher and/or the students can identify current pending legislation that has the potential to affect them.

In small groups, students create a letter to send to their Representatives and Senators asking about their position on the pending bill.

The following are good sites to begin researching legislative contacts:

- U.S. House of Representatives, at www.house.gov
- U.S. Senate, at www.senate.gov
- Open Congress, at www.opencongress.org

The letters should include offers to help with any "on the ground" research and an invitation to visit the class either in person or via videoconference.

The students should track the progress of the bill frequently. The Congressional Record can be accessed from 1994 through the present at http://www.gpoaccess.gov/crecord/index.html.

Presentation

The students can post legislative updates on their class Web site with links to the House and Senate sites.

Variation

The above can be done on a more local level as well. The local mayor, school board president, city or town council members, or state representatives can be contacted for local matters.

Linking With Legislators

Read the Linking with Legislators page at http://alpha.musenet.org:81/ community/call_stories/story_madison.html (created by the Madison Metropolitan School District in Madison, Wisconsin) to read about the report that the students in Mrs. Walser's fourth-grade class researched and authored for their state senator, Fred Risser.

Senator Fred Risser of Wisconsin needed basic research for his pending bill about regulating the sale of cigarettes in vending machines.

The list of skills for this one project is impressive: writing, Internet research, community interviews, and mapping.

Best of all, these students learned that they can directly participate in the real work of their communities.

The provided content supports a unit on drugs and tobacco.

As it turns out, the bill did not pass through the senate. However, any lobbyist will tell you that failure on the first attempt is an important lesson in how state government works.

MANAGING FEAR

As is happening in the broader world of business, information and communication technologies will enable a massive shift of control from the organization to the customer. In the case of education, the shift in control will be from the organization (the school or district) to the client (the learner and the learner's family). It is only natural that a shift of control creates fear and anxiety. Trepidation and fear attend any change, good or bad. The change that comes with the increased and more pervasive use of technology is not what elicits the most fear, although many might think so. The real fear lies in people's hesitancy about the changing roles necessitated by the meaningful use of the technology. It is essential that the fears and anxiety felt by those who are affected by the change not be ignored, but instead be confronted, so that the potential inherent in the change can also be fully explored and realized.

A wonderful activity called *Worst Fears/Best Hopes* can help all teachers face fears and articulate hope at the same time. An individual or group can complete a list of worst fears and then a list of best hopes. See Figure 3.6 for an example of a Worst Fears/Best Hopes list. When in a group, discuss the fears first. Leaders should support and validate every fear and talk about strategies that can be used to minimize realization of the fears. When possible, make the connection between a fear, such as "the loss of social skills," to a hope, such as "we can now connect more students to people around the world." In this way, a map of moving from fear to hope can be generated. The connected lists can become an important document that can be revisited every year to make sure that the fears of the faculty are not coming true. Research suggests that adults will attend a workshop and listen for confirmation of their fears. If fears are articulated, validated, and discussed, adults are in a better position to learn new skills.

Figure 3.6   Worst Fears/Best Hopes

Worst Fears

- o Less physical activity
- o Demand for increased instant gratification
- o E-mail pressures for quick responses that may lack careful contemplation
- o Blurring the lines between professional and private life
- o Rising costs for uses of technology
- o PC use increases the expectation for perfection
- o Addiction to use of technology
- o Increased accentuation between haves and have-nots
- o Increase in destructive hacking
- o Dealing with stress and mental breakdowns as a result of information overload
- o Increased feeling of being less socially active and more isolated
- o Danger in the abundance of inappropriate material available
- o No privacy and a loss of personal identity
- o Loss of the capacity to judge information and an increase in deferring to the computer
- o A loss of caring and sense of community
- o PC use may create a loss of reality
- o A decrease in interpersonal relationships
- o A loss of enjoyment in the simple pleasures
- o A loss of family values and a dehumanization of one's world
- o Computers could control humans
- o Not being able to keep up with information and people
- o Alienation of our youth
- o Others may be in a position to control our future
- o Becoming dependent on technology
- o Colleges may become obsolete

Best Hopes

- o All will learn better, faster, and more
- o Technology will be the equalizer regardless of social status and income
- o People will work more efficiently and have more leisure time
- o Increased exploration of micro and macro worlds
- o Increased opportunities to celebrate our students' work with their communities
- o Teachers will share ideas and knowledge

(Continued)

Figure 3.6 (Continued)

- o Families will be more connected to their children's learning
- o Students will develop more sensitivity to people around the world
- o Expensive educational material will become available to all learners
- o Students will be able to access courses beyond their own communities
- o Better travel opportunities to more countries for our children
- o Supportive society
- o Increase in adaptive technologies resulting in no disabilities
- o Expedite tasks with minimal errors
- o Greater productivity
- o Time savings
- o More comprehensive learning opportunities
- o Increased communications
- o No more drudge work

PROFESSIONAL GROWTH OPPORTUNITY

Relate and Reflect on Chapter 3

The following questions are intended to further promote discussion about learning in planning boards, department meetings, school board meetings, and inservice preparation. They do not require any technological skill or expertise to answer. Space is provided after each question so that you may begin to answer them here. Remember that there is no right or wrong answer.

- Which collegial relationships add value to student work or to the knowledge and skill of the teacher?

- Can teachers within the district form new partnerships based on sharing work?

- Are there potential partnerships that can be nurtured beyond the school district?

- What are the new roles of teachers and students?

- How much control can be shifted from teachers to students to manage learning?

- What are the emerging collaborative relationships for teachers?

Accessing Primary Sources to Enhance Critical Thinking

4

USING PRIMARY SOURCES

As the widow of Jackie Robinson, the first African American to play baseball in the U.S. major leagues, Rachel Robinson must have some amazing stories and insights into the civil rights movement and what it means for an African American female to take a bold stand against prevalent societal norms. Wouldn't you like to get in touch with her and ask for her help in assessing how your students have analyzed the issues of the civil rights movement? I have met teachers who have. Each one began by introducing his or her students to the primary source material on civil rights found on the National Archives site. One teacher was able to reach Rachel Robinson.

While it is not feasible for every teacher in America to ask Rachel Robinson about her experience with civil rights, the core idea of providing students with authentic feedback can be managed in every classroom. Senior citizens, World War II veterans, and students in Israel and Palestine are available with a few clicks. Imagine the impact on student motivation and how the way we teach and learn would change if we could extend access to primary source material and authentic learning relationships!

National Archives and Records Administration (NARA)

Lee Ann Potter is a former classroom teacher who has access to the most amazing primary source documents in the world. She is part of a team of professional educators and archivists at the National Archives and Records Administration (NARA) in Washington, DC. NARA, an independent federal agency that houses and manages all permanently valuable federal records, is developing a Web site to provide public electronic access to thousands of these documents. Potter's work involves digging through billions of documents stored in thousands of boxes on hundreds of miles of shelves to find the most intriguing primary source material to inspire students to want to "do" history and to respect the discipline of history. Building on an education program that has been in place for more than 20 years, Potter develops online curricular materials and conducts teacher workshops. These workshops emphasize how teaching with primary source material can help students value the skills of the historian—asking important questions, seeking clues, constructing hypotheses, and presenting to authentic audiences. Although the Web site is missing the musty basement smell and the feel of leather and old paper, students do not mind. It is the access, authenticity, and sense of uncovering the puzzle pieces that is important. As Potter says, "If we give them access to these documents over the Net, they will be more inclined to visit the Archives when they are in Washington, DC, or one of our other facilities across the country."

The Digital Classroom

When Lee Ann Potter and her colleagues have amassed the material, it becomes part of the Digital Classroom of the National Archives, at http://www.archives.gov/education. One of the most useful teaching resources on the Internet, the Digital Classroom opens worlds beyond the traditional textbook. As Potter wryly observes, "Primary source material was not generated with a grade level or textbook chapter in mind." The Digital Classroom provides educators and students with primary source material and with tools for using primary sources in the classroom. The material is the stuff real historians live for. Now that we have the Internet, it only makes sense to make the collection available to teachers and students. The Digital Classroom's resources can provide teachers with a wonderful organization of primary source evidence and classroom activities. Each unit is linked to the national standards of U.S. history and civics. Units are organized chronologically, from the Constitutional Convention of 1787 to Watergate. The Digital Classroom focuses on U.S. history; however, teachers across the disciplines can use the material to add depth and powerful story lines to the lessons of other subjects.

Using Historical Material in Language Arts

Language arts teachers can use historical material provided in the Digital Classroom that supports teaching novels such as *Little House on the Prairie*.

In a unit called "Little House in the Census: Almanzo and Laura Ingalls Wilder," census records of the Wilder family are highlighted to reveal insights into the real-life details of the book's characters. The information briefly tallied in the census reports gives us glimpses of the drama so richly and lovingly expanded upon by Laura Ingalls Wilder in her tales.

For example, in the 1880 census, the records show that Mary, Laura's sister, was blind, but provided "help in keeping house." Enumerators in that census were instructed not to make such a note unless a daughter "contributed substantially to the welfare of the household."

By linking the research skills of understanding census data with reading Ingalls' books, teachers can help their students to understand the relationship of fact and fiction.

Archival Research Catalog (ARC)

Another NARA initiative involves an online catalog of all Washington, DC holdings, regional records, and presidential libraries.

This catalog is the *Archival Research Catalog (ARC)*. ARC is a searchable database that provides information and digital copies of thousands of primary source documents. The documents ARC has made available online are a very small portion of NARA's holdings; it is not anticipated that all of the archives' holdings will ever be available online due to financial and logistical constraints. Currently, NARA is responsible for billions of items (and constantly growing!), but only 124,000 items—still a considerable cache—are currently online. In addition to the curriculum materials available in the Digital Classroom section of the NARA Web site, educators and students also find the ARC database to be of great value. While traditional curriculum often provides students with exactly the "right" amount of information offered in the "right" order to take the next test, primary source material provides a colorful mosaic with many of the tiles missing or broken. Some of the information will never be found, and sometimes the amount of located information is overwhelming. The fun and the adventure of learning are in the hunt: finding as many pieces as possible, sorting them out, and building defensible patterns of evidence. Potter relates one of her recent experiences:

> I was conducting a workshop for a group of eighth-grade students enrolled in a cyber camp at Howard University a few summers ago. I was introducing them to ARC's prototype. I reminded them that all of the documents held by the National Archives are those of the federal government. I asked them to search for documents in the database using the names of significant people that they knew had something to do with the government in our nation's past. One young man searched on "George Bush." One of the documents he retrieved was a page from the *USS San Jacinto's* logbook, dated September 2, 1944. It mentioned that a plane had been shot down, but that a submarine had rescued its pilot, a G. H. W. Bush. I told the student that he'd found a very interesting document. He agreed that it was interesting, but unfortunately it was not the George Bush he had been looking for. You see, he had been searching for documents related to President [G. H. W.] Bush, not some World War II pilot. I asked the student if he was sure they weren't one and the same—he was convinced that they couldn't be. So, I sent him to some other sources for biographical information on President Bush. When he realized that President Bush had indeed been a naval pilot, it was exciting for both of us. For him, the document encouraged him to conduct further research and find out information on his own. For me, the episode

reinforced the power of primary sources in not just teaching historical content, but also in encouraging valuable research skills.

Using Historical Material in Science

Challenge science students to research historical artifacts as a key element in understanding the impact of human behavior and the fragile balance of environmental systems.

The NARA Web site has a link to FirstGov at http://www.usa.gov/, which is an extensive directory of government agencies that, among other information resources, link to numerous scientific research sites.

An important part of this story is that Lee Ann Potter was there as a thoughtful educator who was able to lead a student to further research of primary source material. As we gain access to more primary sources, the role of the teacher will become increasingly more important than when textbooks were the medium of information for students. Students often do not see connections between primary source material, such as the World War II submarine logbook referring to G. H. W. Bush, and their desire to search for a source, such as President G. H. W. Bush. In some cases, we will have to teach students to let go of the notion that the answers are more important than the questions and the process. Eventually, textbooks will only be used as another reference rather than the dominant media. While providing the material on the Web is invaluable, the role of the teacher is more important than ever in helping students to learn to think critically. Teachers can record observations of student use of primary sources by using the questions in Figure 4.1.

Figure 4.1 Questions for Using Primary Sources

- Do students understand the definition of a primary source?
- Do students have the skills to document the source of the primary source?
- Do students have a well-defined search strategy?
- Do students know when to use different search engines and databases?
- Do students have the ability to make meaning from the primary sources that they found?
- Are students easily distracted or do they stay on task?

(Continued)

Figure 4.1 (Continued)

- Do different students have different strategies?
- Where are students struggling?
- Where are they delighted?
- Are they using their imagination (e.g., asking "what if" questions)?
- Which students are taking the lead?
- Are the girls as involved as the boys? Are the boys as involved as the girls?
- What is the role of the instructor when student(s) ask for help?
- Are students working well together?

The Archivists

While the technical skill of accessing the archives via e-mail or the Web is easy, teaching students to carefully focus their questions and communications can be more difficult. One of the features of the NARA Web site is that students can send their questions to an archivist. Some of this correspondence can cause bewilderment and a few chuckles. Imagine that you are working in a building with millions of documents. How would you respond to this student's request: "Please, I have to write a paper, due next week. Can you send me everything you have about the Civil War? Hurry!"

Teaching students to develop thoughtful and precise questions about history or a scientific development is essential.

The *E-VENTURE* below is based on material for establishing a school archive developed by NARA. Students are provided with the opportunity to create a repository of historically significant artifacts and papers with the help of peers and outside experts. Additional information about creating archives is available from the NARA Web site, at www.archives.gov/about/history/building-an-archives/school-archives.html.

E-VENTURE: Do-It-Yourself School Archives

Purpose: to stimulate students to explore the concepts of local history and conservancy; to make real-world and timely connections between the present day and a time period in the past; to teach research-related skills

Investigation

1. The teacher and the students identify people willing to support the creation of a school archive. These people might include the principal, the

teacher in the building or district with the most tenure, local residents, staff from a local college or university, and staff from the town's historical society or library.

2. Determine, in conjunction with supporting people, what the class hopes to accomplish.

3. Select a physical location to house the materials.

4. Elect or appoint an archivist.

5. Determine what equipment and supplies are needed.

6. Prepare a budget for the project.

7. Draft rules and regulations.

8. Create teams to collect oral history interviews, evaluate documents for inclusion, conduct research, scan or otherwise digitize images, and catalog materials using spreadsheet and database programs.

Presentation

Once the collection is established, the class as a whole can design a Web site to post digitized images with descriptions.

OR

Students can plan and implement an online video event in which the contents of the archive are presented. The presentation may also be video recorded for broadcast on the local cable station.

Variation

Instead of creating a school archive, each student can create a family or personal archive. Experts used in this case might include the family doctor, clergy, and other family members.

If an archive already exists at your school, students can help determine, with the help of the archivist, what can be done to make the collection more accessible to students and others.

Items to Collect for School Archives

- Student handbooks
- Student newspapers
- Yearbooks

(Continued)

(Continued)

- Photographs
- School lunch menus
- Course catalogs
- Rare textbooks
- Student term papers about the school and community
- Artifacts (e.g., trophies, flags, uniforms, donated objects, memorabilia)
- Newspaper articles from the local newspaper
- Special awards received by the school
- Records of special school programs

TEACHING THE SKILLS TO ASSESS PRIMARY SOURCES

One of my favorite units in NARA's Digital Classroom is about civil rights. Jackie Robinson is a familiar icon to millions of children. Even people who do not follow baseball probably know that he was the first player to cross the color barrier in professional sports when he joined the Brooklyn Dodgers. What many students may not know is that he was very active in the civil rights movement from the 1950s until his death in 1972. His letters to four presidents—Eisenhower, Kennedy, Johnson, and Nixon—provide an inside view of how one African American felt about the approach of four different administrations. The archives also include correspondence back to Robinson from the presidents who answered his letters. As with many primary sources, though, the material raises more questions than answers. While the letters provide a fascinating glimpse into history, students can be overwhelmed when asked to make sense of them in terms of their importance to the civil rights movement. Many students have not been taught to develop strategies for thinking about and evaluating primary sources. The role of the teacher is to provide structure and direction to a student's ability to make meaning.

> Are we just telling students to go to the search engines when they research on the Web, or are we helping them to focus their search on where to go? We would not send students into a physical library and say, "Wander around until you find something interesting." Nor should we be sending students to the Web and then simply say, "Go."
>
> —*Lee Ann Potter, NARA, Washington, DC*

Perspective

One of the most important skills that students should learn is to understand the language and perspective of the organization or the people who provide primary source material. For example, Lee Ann Potter worked with students as they used ARC, the professional online database of the NARA, to search for "Trail of Tears." While these students were using a common phrase—"Trail of Tears"—to search for information about the forced march of the Cherokee from their homelands in North Carolina to Oklahoma, it did not yield results in ARC. "Of course, the students did not find what they were hoping for with those keywords and they were frustrated." Potter goes on to explain, "Would the federal government have called the removal of the Cherokee the 'Trail of Tears'?" Probably not. The search may have been more productive if students searched for "Indian removal." Students did not think from the government's perspective.

Database Search Skills

Teaching students to play with search terms and to think about the subtleties of words is also important. When you search with the word *airplane*, you do not get the same results as when searching with the word *aircraft*. Students do not necessarily come prepared with the discipline and rigor of crafting a successful search. The important pedagogy is to teach students to think about bias and subtleties. While it is important to provide students with structure, it can also be very important to allow students to fail with ill-conceived searches. Feeling the frustration of continued failed searches and then finding success can be very empowering for students.

Almost Like Being There

Virtual tours of facilities such as the Smithsonian, the Metropolitan Museum of Art, and the Louvre give students the chance to glimpse the treasures that they might otherwise never be able to see. Scott M. Mandel's (1999) book *Virtual Field Trips in the Cyberage: A Content Mapping Approach* gives a number of well-planned virtual trips to these and other cyber destinations, including curricular connections.

Visual Literacy

Most Americans are inundated with massive amounts of visual stimuli. Special effects can make anything seem real. It is more important than ever for students to be equipped with the skill set necessary to sort fact from fiction. Visual literacy is as important as the ability to critically examine text.

E-VENTURE: What's Wrong With This Picture: Adventures in Visual Literacy

Purpose: to help students use science knowledge to make sense of visual stimuli

Investigation

1. The class watches a portion of a movie or television show with a science fiction theme, such as *Star Wars* or *2001: A Space Odyssey*.

2. While viewing the material, the students note what is taking place that is scientifically impossible. For example, many space epics have huge and fiery space explosions with terrific bursts of sound, but because space is a vacuum, it would not be possible to hear an explosion. The class is debriefed after the screening to determine what aspects of the movie they thought might be scientifically unsound.

3. The students form groups of three or four.

4. Each group investigates whether the dubious cinematic depiction holds up by designing an experiment that would prove or disprove the vision in the movie.

Presentation

Each small group performs their experiment for the class.

Variation

Language arts students could view a movie and compare it to the book version. Students should discuss why the visual medium differs from the text version. They should form an opinion about which was better and why. Students should determine if material was left out or added to the movie version. They should also decide if it is important for a movie to be true to the novel or book and give reasons for their answer. Books that can easily be examined and that are often already woven into the curriculum are *The Miracle Worker* and *Willy Wonka and the Chocolate Factory*.

In a social science class, a movie based on a particular time in history can be examined for its historical accuracy.

Thinking Critically About Primary Source Material

Teachers can help students learn to evaluate primary sources. Students should critically question the primary source documents they encounter. Teachers can guide students through the questioning process until they are able to formulate questions independently. Students should also look for other documents related to the primary source material. These other information sources will either refute or support answers to students' critical questions, as well as offer new information for further research. The evaluation process will not only help students analyze the primary sources, it will also help students organize what may be overwhelming material.

Generating Questions

Questions can be used to probe students' thinking skills when they are evaluating primary sources. For example, questions to ask about the Jackie Robinson letters include the following:

- What prompted Robinson to write the letters and telegrams?
- What is a telegram?
- What were his expectations?
- What happened that provoked Robinson to write?
- How did each administration deal with civil rights?
- Why was he so upset with Kennedy and pleased with Nixon?
- Which president did Robinson believe was the most progressive?

Encouraging students to focus on a specific question can help them analyze their primary document. In the case of Jackie Robinson, students might ask which of the four presidents Robinson believed to be the most progressive concerning civil rights.

Identifying Information Sources

Encouraging students to examine other information sources is a good way to help them learn more about their primary sources. Asking students what other primary sources can be accessed to help make meaning out of what was found in the archives can help them to begin their research. For the Jackie Robinson material, the teacher might suggest searching sources such as the congressional record or news accounts of the day. Another way to help students get more information about primary sources is to prompt them to explore organizations that can help them make meaning of the documents. In the case of Jackie Robinson, students could explore the local

NAACP, the Martin Luther King Center, and the Major League Players Association.

Student-Generated Data

Students need not rely on outside sources to solve problems. They can collect the data they need using simple technology tools. As is the case with information found on the Internet, the real learning begins when the data that has been collected is analyzed. Sources of data collection can take various forms, including counting cars through an intersection and using spreadsheet software to display data. A PDA (personal digital assistant) can be used to store data as it is being collected. Students can also use probes in the way my daughter once did.

Jessie's Story

Wavelength Probe

My daughter, Jessie, grabbed a PalmPilot and hooked it up to a light probe. She and her friend had a hypothesis that the individual colors that make up white light would have different wavelengths. She needed a tool to record the wavelengths. The PalmPilot with the right software, ImagiWorks, and a light probe made a very powerful and easy-to-use light wave recorder. The probe was designed so students could easily construct light filters of various colors. She dashed off to the business supply store to buy colored plastic folders to cut into filters. Then she and her friend taped down the light probe, attached it to the PalmPilot, and turned her bedroom into a physics lab. The two of them were in a zone—as in "We can do it, Daddy"—building the filters and taking measurements. Within a few hours they had recorded the wavelengths for blue, green, and red light. The next step was to synchronize the PalmPilot with the computer and move the data into Excel (I did get to help with this step.) so that graphs could be printed for the final report. They had the data to show that the hypothesis was valid.

Of course, Jessie could have read about the wavelengths of different colors. But I am convinced that her understanding of wavelengths is deeper because she was able to construct her own experiment. When I was her age, it would not have been financially feasible to build a tool for measuring light waves. I had to wait until I was in high school to look at the physics of light waves. The *flow* kids experience when they have the tools at hand to construct their own hypotheses, test them, and report on them makes giving them access to these tools compelling. (The idea of *flow* comes from Csikszentmihalyi, 1991.)

Experts

Access to experts sets the stage for students to become self-reliant in terms of meaning-making and confident in their own power to make connections and find the answers to their questions. Experts and students become *partners in cognition* (Saloman, Perkins, & Globerson, 1991). Professors, government officials, attorneys, physicians, and museum curators are just some of the experts with whom students can connect to gain information and understanding on a particular topic. By corresponding or conversing with an expert, students can get the most up-to-date thinking about a particular topic or the answers to questions they could not find elsewhere. A face-to-face interview with a local author and a student or group of students, or an e-mail correspondence with an author in another locale, promotes student interest and makes the concepts of writing and reading seem like more productive enterprises. Teachers can help facilitate such connections through Web sites. Do not underestimate the power of peers as potential sources of expert information. Teachers can help students connect with peers across town or across the globe to see how they handled a particular project. Chances are, once you show your students what others have accomplished, they will want to create something even more powerful.

Finding an Authentic Audience for Student Analysis

Once students have completed an analysis of the primary source material, students can find an authentic audience to review their work. An authentic audience can provide additional information to help inform a student about the meaning of a primary source document as well as give feedback. Many students will work harder for an authentic audience than for their own teacher. For the Jackie Robinson project, contact the local NAACP to see if they would review excerpts from your class. Since it can be very difficult for an authentic audience to evaluate every student's work, have the class vote for the best analysis or edit student conclusions into one document to be presented to the authentic audience.

E-VENTURE: Kennedy Versus Nixon, October 13, 1960

Purpose: to guide students to critically evaluate primary source documents

Investigation

In three groups, students are assigned to examine the third Kennedy-Nixon debate. One group is assigned to watch a video; one group listens to an audio recording; and one group reads the transcript of the debate. For information, see the following sources:

- The American Presidency Project (Transcript available of the third debate) http://www.presidency.ucsb.edu/showdebate.php?debateid=3
- The Internet Archive (Audio available of the third debate) http://www.archive.org/audio/xspf_player.php?collectionid=Kennedy-Nixon_third_debate_10_13_1960

Guided by the teacher, the class as a whole brainstorms criteria for critically evaluating each candidate's performance.

Presentation

After evaluating the assigned material, each group develops a report that will be posted on the class Web site. Each group should also prepare a flowchart showing the course of the debate.

After each of the presentations, the class should discuss and formulate hypotheses regarding why each group has made the determinations they have. They should discuss what factors influence a person's credibility and ability to communicate and connect with people.

NARA Worksheets

The educational staff of the NARA has developed a number of analysis worksheets that help students or any researchers evaluate primary source material. The worksheets can be accessed and printed for classroom use at www.archives.gov/education/lessons/. Brief summaries of the worksheets are provided in the following paragraphs and illustrated in Figures 4.2 and 4.3.

The Written Document Analysis Worksheet (see Figure 4.2) asks students to list the document's author, date, genre, unique physical qualities, and intended audience. Students also answer critical questions, such as why they think the document was written.

| Figure 4.2 | Screenshot of NARA's Written Document Analysis Worksheet |

The *Photograph Analysis Worksheet* 1 asks students to study a photograph and form an overall impression. Students are also asked to study individual elements and record observations.

Figure 4.3 Screenshots Depicting NARA's Analysis Worksheets

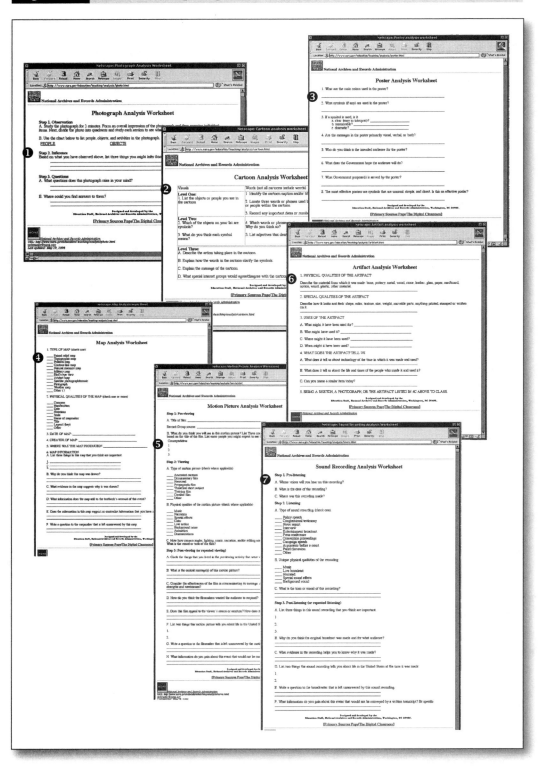

The *Cartoon Analysis Worksheet* 2 asks students to analyze the visual and written elements on three levels. Level 1 asks for a list of elements, Level 2 asks for an evaluation of elements, and Level 3 asks for critical response to elements.

The *Poster Analysis Worksheet* 3 asks students to list and respond to the poster's colors, symbols, messages, purpose, and effectiveness.

The *Map Analysis Worksheet* 4 asks students to list the map's creator, date, type, physical qualities, and production location. Students are also asked to evaluate the map's purpose and information and provide evidence for their answers.

The *Motion Picture Analysis Worksheet* 5 asks students to list the film's title and source and predict the content and concepts before viewing. During viewing, students are asked to list the film's genre, physical qualities, and mood. After repeated viewing, students are also asked to support their predictions and state the film's theme, effectiveness, and appeal.

The *Artifact Analysis Worksheet* 6 asks students to list the artifact's physical qualities, special features, and uses.

The *Sound Recording Analysis Worksheet* 7 asks students to list the date, voices, and recording location before listening. During listening, students are asked to list the recording's type, unique physical qualities, and mood. After repeated listening, students are also asked to state the recording's purpose and important qualities.

PROFESSIONAL GROWTH OPPORTUNITY

Relate and Reflect on Chapter 4

The following questions are intended to further and promote discussion about learning in planning boards, department meetings, school board meetings, and inservice preparation. They do not require any technological skill or expertise to answer. Space is provided after each question so that you may begin to answer them here. Remember that there is no right or wrong answer.

• What is the right balance between giving students freedom to explore the Web for research and providing them with structure and guidance?

• What is the role of the teacher in helping students to make meaning of primary source material?

Online Learning **5**

In the 2001 first edition of this book, this chapter began with a prediction: "Of all the potential technology holds, learning online may have the greatest impact on the education system. The potential benefits of providing learning opportunities anytime, anywhere, to anybody, are provocative."

The impact of online learning is no longer a prediction. At the time of the first printing in 2001, only 45,000 students enrolled in an online course. Online learning was a mere blip on the radar screen. In 2007, that blip became fuller and stronger as K–12 online student enrollment topped 1,000,000. Technological advancements and social trends, such as students moving to online social networks such as Facebook, and a decline in financial resources now make online learning a potential strategic planning tool for any U.S. school district. There is also a huge incentive in Asia and Europe for access to online courses. Perhaps the most outrageous predictions in the growth curve of online learning are by Harvard Business School professor Clayton M. Christensen. In his 2008 book, *Disrupting Class: How Disruptive Innovation Will Change the Way the World Learns* (Christensen, Horn, & Johnson, 2008), more than half of all high school courses will be delivered online by 2019.

Online learning initiatives are thriving today, created behind the idea that schools and districts can pool resources to provide services and courses to a wide range of learners. The benefits of online learning extend to the homebound student and the home schooled student. They also benefit the AP (Advanced Placement) student in a small high school that cannot offer every AP course to those rural students who are geographically isolated. For those families who believe their children are gifted and can afford the price, Stanford University has launched www.epgy.org. EPGY (Education Program for Gifted Youth) courses begin in kindergarten and extend through university offerings.

Online learning is also growing very fast as an option for professional development. Many teachers who do not have the time to take after school workshops can tap into a rich array of professional development offerings from their home or from their own classroom. Cell phone manufacturers are predicting that small mobile devices will become the tool of choice for online learning—anywhere, anytime.

Online learning is made practical by the increase in bandwidth and the decrease in the cost of technology. Powerful and easy-to-use open source tools such as Moodle (www.moodle.org) are making the design and delivery of online courses as easy as using a word processor.

The debate is no longer about *if* we will have online learning; it is too late to stop it because there is a massive movement by universities and colleges to build entire degrees online. In addition, private industry has discovered the cost saving value and power of online meeting software such as Illuminate,

WEBex, and GoToMeeting. These systems can tap networks of talent to focus on problem solving or to deliver real-time professional development. Online meetings and online learning have become an essential 21st-century skill. Eventually, many of our students will need to learn how to manage their learning with people who are not sitting next to them in a classroom. Elite U.S. universities, such as Stanford and MIT, have made a commitment to publish professor's lectures and course materials online. (See http://www.apple.com/education/mobile-learning/ for more information.)

One of the sad ironies of school filtering is that some of the most amazing free resources for online learning are available at sites that are blocked, such as iTunesU. Too many schools are blocking courses from Duke, MIT, and Stanford from reaching K–12 school campuses.

Do schools have an obligation to prepare students for a world where those who can access learning resources 24-7 potentially have an enormous advantage over those who can only rely on the physical structure of the classroom to learn?

Understandably, everyone in the education community has not met online learning with equal enthusiasm. Some bemoan the loss of the social interaction of both students and teachers. The quality of curriculum is questioned, and issues of state certification and local control are used to prevent courses from crossing state or national boundaries. In many ways, while the concerns are real, the fear of loss of control may be blocking opportunities for students and teachers to gain access to valuable learning resources.

The United States is no longer the leader in online design resources for K–12. Scotland is building a nationwide online learning platform called Glow (http://www.ltscotland.org.uk/glowscotland/index.asp). This platform will link every school together for the benefit of sharing resources for learning for both pupils and professional development. Teachers will have tools for creating online groups, interactive online whiteboards, and professional communities for sharing resources. Every primary and secondary student will have access. Marie Dougan, Glow Program Director, explains that the social networking tools of Glow are already familiar to her own three teenage children. Laurie O'Donnell, director of Learning and Technology for Scotland, shares that "Glow was launched with the expectation that it would provide Scottish learners and teachers with the best resources in the world for learning and teaching." Where is the United States?

PIONEERS ON THE DIGITAL FRONTIER

The experiences of the administrators, teachers, and students at three online schools show how 24-7 learning looks in practice and how pioneering efforts pave the way for expanded opportunities. The following are among the pioneering institutions of online education:

Pioneering Online Schools

- Electronic High School (EHS), Utah, Richard Siddoway, principal
  http://ehs.uen.org
- The Florida Virtual School (FLVS), headed by Julie Young
  http://www.flvs.net/
- The Virtual High School (VHS), Concord Consortiums, headed by Liz Pape
  http://www.govhs.org

Each school built programs from the ground up, tailoring the course offerings to the student and to the medium—the Internet. The lessons that were learned from these online ventures and the comments from administrators, teachers, parents, and the students who were involved are included throughout this chapter.

A World Away From the Desktop

Although VHS is a virtual high school, it actively encourages students to get away from the computers. Serving students from some 457 schools in 28 states and 35 foreign countries, VHS definitely does not want students doing every scrap of work in front of a computer monitor. The first VHS head, Bruce Droste, made this alignment very clear when he said, "It doesn't all have to be Internet based. It could be, 'Go out and interview somebody. Come back. Share with us what that interview is.' A lot of what we're trying to do is have these courses act as springboards away from the machines. We don't want this to be, well, what some people would call 'heads-down' learning."

Well, if it is great academically, and it is also not going to cause social disadvantages, should everyone take every course online? The answer from those involved with VHS was "no." Droste summed up what everyone in VHS thought when he presented both a philosophical and physical argument against taking a full load online:

> We also have a requirement that students cannot make the VHS their entire course load. We won't let that happen. I believe, and everyone on my team believes, that you need the handshake and

the hug. You need to bump into the student in the hall. You have to have that personal contact. People need to know how to act face-to-face with one another. I mean, where are we headed? The Virtual Prom? That will never happen!

Academy On-line made sure that it set up multiple occasions online and offline for students and adults to socialize. Each school year began with an inservice day that everyone attended in order to get their computers from the school. Parents, teachers, and the principal sat down together to talk about the upcoming year. Meanwhile, the students went downstairs to hang out and get to know one another. When I heard about this, I thought back to my high school. In my mind, I selected 100 students, the same number of students enrolled in Academy On-line. Did I know those students' favorite cars? Their favorite movies? Their favorite subjects in school? If I had possessed that knowledge, think of the conversations I could have started and the friends I could have made. The students of Academy On-line had that opportunity—and often made the most of it. Students' willingness to make connections is evidence that the Internet does not blunt our inborn need to socialize with other humans. If anything, the Internet facilitates that need to socialize like no other tool we've ever had.

One fear of most opponents of online learning is that the quality of education will be sacrificed. The National Education Association (NEA) has addressed this concern by sharing their belief that "each constituent in the online education process (policymakers, administrators, teachers, parents, and students) must consider a number of important issues when contemplating creating, adopting, administering, or participating in online courses" (National Education Association [NEA], 2002).

Figure 5.1 Quality Distance Learning

To ensure quality, distance education courses must

- Be at least as rigorous as similar courses delivered by more traditional means
- Meet accreditation standards
- Present content that is relevant, is accurate, meets state and local standards, and is subject to the normal processes of collegial decision making
- Meet the objectives and requirements outlined in the official course description

(Continued)

Figure 5.1	(Continued)

- Maintain student/faculty ratios that ensure the active engagement of students and high academic achievement
- Have appropriate procedures mutually agreed upon by the instructor and the institution for evaluation and verification that the student is submitting his or her own work
- Employ instructors whose qualifications are the same as those instructors in traditional classes and who are prepared specifically and comprehensively to teach in this environment
- Be integrated into the mission and consistent with the overall offerings of the institution
- Provide fair use exemption for participants' access to copyrighted material for educational purposes

CHANGING ROLES AND INTERACTIONS

At its core, online learning means that the role of the teacher, the responsibility of the student, the relationships between school and home, and the traditional boundaries of school departments, grades, and schedules will become much more permeable. Our current concepts of time, space, and relationships will shift. For those who can take advantage of these changes and learn to manage the flow of learning online, there will be powerful new opportunities. In many ways, we have an opportunity to rethink why so many students claim to be bored and why so few ever achieve the highest levels of academic achievement. Online learning will affect many facets of education delivery and philosophy, including the

- Role of the student
- Role of the teacher
- Role of the family
- Management of public dollars
- Equity of access

Positive Student Interaction

Some students feel safer expressing themselves online. "My online high school course is the first class that four of my students have ever participated in. One student said, 'I like being anonymous,'" explains Ruth Williams, a staff development specialist with the Chesterfield County Public Schools in Richmond, Virginia. Students have time to respond, so they can be more thoughtful in their answers, and they cannot see other students rolling their eyes or laughing at something they said. This kind of safe atmosphere allows some students to really push themselves intellectually and express themselves without fear of recrimination. The anonymity of online learning really brings out learning as an adventure for some students. Droste suggests it is because no one can tell by your online conversation that you are overweight, have zits, or wear braces. Maybe it is because, as a former VHS student Jon Timner volunteers, "You're not penalized for trying something different. Other students don't make fun of you for putting in effort."

Improved Teacher Interaction

Whether online or off, genuine communication between a teacher and a student is critical. Social relationships between teachers and students can be just as meaningful online as they are offline, if not more so. Many students reported that they received more feedback from their online teachers. Further, a large number of online students also believe that they know their online teacher better than any teacher in the school building. This change in the relationship between teacher and student even carries over into the brick and mortar classroom. Many students are now more likely to ask questions and demand attention in their other classes because their experience online has empowered them.

Peer Interaction on the Internet

Much as we may be glad for improved relations between teachers and their students, it is the relations between peers that most concern us. How do students interact online with other students? And why are students so interested in interacting via the Internet? For one thing, it is the lure of the exotic.

Another reason students are interested in the Internet is because they are all in it together. It is hard to exclude each other when you are learning online. Former VHS student Timner supports that. "There aren't any cliques at VHS. No one limited his or her comments to just another two or three students. Everyone commented on everyone else's work." In an online learning environment, a student has to reach out and work with his or her fellow classmates. Richard Siddoway of EHS put it best: "To be successful, you cannot be a hermit."

Ultimately, students enjoy working on the Internet because the highly collaborative environment the students work in means that they come to rely on each other and learn what each other think and believe. Another VHS student said about her peers, "I know about their ideas. There's not as much sharing of ideas in a regular classroom setting. Everything is superficial [in] an ordinary classroom—it's about noticing how others act, what they look like." Since virtually everything a student does is on display, students develop a sense of each other that brings with it emotional closeness. And they can judge each other only on the basis of those ideas, not on looks. Timner impressed me when he pointed out, "You can know someone just by what's inside them, by the comments they say and that type of thing, instead of thinking, 'Ooo, that person looks weird.'"

Better Parent Interaction

It was not just interactions between students that were improved by virtual learning. Some students also got to know their parents better as well. Several of the parents wanted to see what their children's online school looked like, and the students eagerly obliged. Parents also reported that even children who did not normally share homework were showing them their work, even when the parents did not ask. Leigh Gilahen happily asserted after her daughter took a VHS online music course, "This is something we can all kind of share. I think that's good. There's not a lot of things around that prompt that kind of 'Hey, everyone, come see this.'"

STUDENTS INVOLVED IN ONLINE LEARNING

Students who succeed online are not the uniformly gifted or academically engaged students we might expect. In fact, it is precisely the gifted or academically engaged students who may dislike the experience of Internet classes the most. It may seem odd, but students who failed courses while they were sitting in classrooms can do particularly well with online courses. See Figure 5.2 for students who are likely to enroll in online classes.

Figure 5.2   Students Who Enroll in Online Learning Classes

- Students who have failed a class, must make up credit, and need another option to taking the make-up class during the summer or after school
- Students who want to take a class not offered at school, especially when the school is so remote that it has only a few teachers
- Students who want to graduate early by earning extra credits outside their regular schooling
- Students who are home schooled
- International students from as far away as Siberia
- Adults who want to learn new things
- Dropouts studying for a GED
- Students isolated because of an illness or disability
- Younger students who want to participate in more challenging learning experiences

Who Makes a Good Online Student

Students of varying abilities can do well online. In fact, students tend to get better grades in their online courses than they do in regular classes, and it is not because the classes online are easier. Motivation to succeed online comes from many different sources. Students who love learning are motivated to do well because that is the kind of people they are. Students who enjoy computers are motivated to do well because they are very comfortable with the medium. But having to complete a course to graduate and getting to do that course work at your own pace can be one heck of a motivator as well! Students who typically succeed at online learning possess the following traits:

- Motivation to take the class
- Self-discipline and responsibility
- The ability to work independently
- Parental support

Motivation to Take the Class

This might seem obvious, but everyone I spoke with involved in online learning had a horror story about a student who was forced to take a despised class online and who proceeded to hate the entire experience before mercifully dropping out. Motivation can come from a student's pure desire to learn, but Siddoway, principal of EHS, reminds us that it can also arise from the need to take a course in order to graduate. In either case, the student wants to take the course and will feel vested in the experience. With proper motivation, students are more likely to succeed, regardless if that success is measured by a passing grade, an "A," or the acquisition of new knowledge and skills.

Self-Discipline and Responsibility

In many face-to-face classrooms, teachers manage the learning of the students. Content, presentation, and discussion move at the speed presented by the teacher. Student behavior is guided word by word. With virtual learning, however, the responsibility of managing information shifts to the learner. It is this sense of personal responsibility that inspires and empowers these students to excel. Many students instinctively embrace this kind of learning and see its advantages. With online learning, students can do their work when they are best prepared mentally and physically to do it, whether that is 9 a.m., 8 p.m., or 2 a.m. Furthermore, if they need more time to do a particular task, they can take as much time as they need. Students can spend all the time they want studying because the materials are there for them online, 24 hours a day, seven days a week.

Some students can complete a semester of class in just a few weeks. If they have the time, and if they have the will, they can zip through the materials. On the other hand, if a student cannot handle the responsibility of managing their own learning, they drop out.

The Ability to Work Independently

Rocky Burrol began taking all of his courses through Academy On-line when he was a seventh grader. When I asked him how his online learning experience differed from his sixth-grade year, he told me, "A major change was having to motivate myself to do my [online] schoolwork." I expressed surprise at this, and I asked him if it was hard for a seventh grader to work independently. He replied, "Not really. I found I like it better because my assignments were more organized. I found

> **Profile of a Successful Online Student**
>
> - Motivated to take the class
> - Self-disciplined and responsible
> - Able to work independently
> - Has parental support

I was more exact. If you were someone who relies on other people more, it would be harder, but if you're motivated, it's not too bad. You have to be self-motivated and able to work by yourself."

Parental Support

The teachers, students, and parents involved in online learning all agreed that parental support is a key requirement for a student taking a class over the Internet. The administrators associated with the three online learning sites all emphatically agreed that parental involvement was exceedingly important and that a lack of parental support could hurt a student's chance for success beyond the hope of recovery. Fortunately, online education seems to draw the parents into the process in ways that regular schooling often does not. In fact, Siddoway, principal of EHS, told me that he has a sneaking suspicion that "this is the first time in a while for many of these parents that they've been involved in their student's education." Whether it is because Internet-based education is perceived as something new and different, or because the classes are necessary for the student to graduate, many parents get involved, and that helps students learn.

Online Learning Is Not Right for Everybody

Some students drop out of online high schools for personal reasons. This type of learning simply is not for them. You may be surprised by how Droste responded when I asked which students disliked VHS. "If there was a group of students who could be characterized as most unhappy with VHS, it was those students who always sit in the front row, middle desk and answer every question." If you think about it, his observation makes sense. These students are used to being the stars in class, often because they are quick-witted and always prepared with a ready answer. In the online classrooms of VHS, where taking your time and coming up with a thoughtful answer is the rule, the stars of the classroom do not always shine as brightly.

Not surprisingly, students do not do well in online learning if they do not really want to be there. One of the VHS teachers described a scene she witnessed at her school, a situation destined to produce failure: "Some counselors schedule a student for a course, but it fills up, so they shove the student into a course he or she isn't interested in. The student starts the course out bitter, and it doesn't get any better. It affects how well the students do." All of us involved in education know how difficult it can be to interest a student who has decided he or she does not like your subject and does not want to be in your classroom. Nothing will transform excited anticipation into sullen disgust like coercing students into studying something that they hate and, worse, know that they have been forced into taking by adults.

According to Siddoway, principal of EHS, around 3% of the students taking a course with EHS do not finish it. The biggest reason students leave EHS? They just do not enjoy learning that way. It is not for them. But overall, most students involved in this program make the transition to learning online handily. They enjoy it. The biggest reason for enjoying EHS lies in the change in time, space, and relationships—when you learn, where you learn, who manages the learning, and the relationship between teachers and students.

> **Successful Online Teachers**
>
> - Think out of the box
> - Are certified to teach in the state
> - Have four or five years of classroom experience
> - Have not taught the same course year after year
> - Like students
> - Are willing to learn and apply what they learn to teaching students
> - Are not technophobes or techies

TEACHERS INVOLVED IN ONLINE LEARNING

The teacher is all-important. There can be no doubt of that. "The teachers make it good," Droste reminds us. "This project is not about technology. It's about access and learning. We're using technology as the delivery method. Students are writing to us saying, 'I want more. This is the best class I've ever taken, because of the teachers, not because of the technology.'"

Who Makes a Good Online Teacher

The teachers who work best online have a lot in common with the students who do their best work there. When VHS was first asking schools to participate, administrators at various schools thought they knew who the best teachers would be, but they were wrong. "The star teacher has become a star in the classroom more often than not because of the way he or she delivers knowledge to students, using body language and tone of voice," Droste says. "In addition, he or she is good at improvisation in the midst of spirited class discussions." Online, such tools and skills become useless. The teacher must rely on written language and a measured, well-thought-out, give-and-take communication instead of a rapid question-and-answer session. Schools providing online courses are not looking for star teachers, but rather for good teachers. Still, each school has its own slant on exactly the teacher it is looking for. All schools seek that elusive and hard-to-define quality exemplified by a "good teacher." In addition to certain personality traits and experience that might attract a person to teaching online, the teacher who is ultimately successful at online teaching also

- Devotes time and energy to teaching online
- Is available to students
- Is creative and willing to experiment
- Breaks down curricula into clearly organized, clearly explained smaller units
- Focuses on concepts, not class periods
- Integrates curricula

Devotes Time and Energy to Teaching Online

Some people are under the impression that teachers who work online have it easier than teachers who work in the classroom. After all, the argument goes, all they have to do is send the students some Web pages and answer a few e-mails. How hard can it be? However, each of the online administrators I spoke with emphasized that online education is, as Siddoway, principal of EHS, put it, "more work than the teachers thought it would be." Even the students thought so! Those participating in online courses, both teachers and students, all emphasized that students get more from the teachers who take the time to really individualize the material and the process of learning.

Available to Students

Online education is essentially asynchronous. For the student, this means that he or she can learn at any time. For the teacher, though, this means having to answer e-mails sent at any time of the day or night. Some teachers set up office hours so students know that they can expect answers only between 8 a.m. and 5 p.m. Others promise a reply within 24 hours. Students need to know they can reach a teacher if they need help or want to discuss an idea.

Creative and Willing to Experiment

VHS specifically wanted risk takers to join its new venture. When it was brand new, VHS wanted people who were willing to fail. The results surprised even some of the teachers who signed up, as demonstrated by one teacher who told Droste, the founding head of VHS, "I didn't think I was a risk taker, but now I know I am."

Things are very different online for the teacher. As most of us who have been online for any length of time know, things seem to proceed more quickly on the Internet. Wayne Poncia, formerly of Academy On-line in Alberta, gave advice that any teacher looking to work online would do well to heed: "Learning is fast and furious. The teacher keeps up with the students rather than the students keeping pace with the teacher."

To work at this fast pace, many things that work in the classroom setting need to be unlearned by the teacher. VHS teacher Lillian Bonekin had to learn this the hard way, but learn it she did. Now she wants to share her experience with other teachers so that they can deal with the transition more easily. "A teacher who just lectures in the classroom would not make a good VHS teacher," she says. "A teacher who's not willing to make changes, who is so into the traditional setting and the traditional grading system and the traditional way of learning would not make the transition easily. The students would not react well. You can't be too traditional in the VHS setting. You have to be creative, and you have to be open."

Breaks Down the Curricula Into Smaller Units

As the teacher moves from the traditional classroom to the electronic classroom, he or she will have to change his or her curricula so that it fits into the new format. Over and over, from administrators, teachers, and students, I heard about the necessity of breaking that curriculum down into smaller units. Once those units are broken down, they must follow a clearly organized, logical progression of thought.

Since teachers are dealing with a variety of students who all learn at different rates, this organization into small units is vitally important. Siddoway, principal of EHS, pointed out, "What is daily size for you may be week size for me." If students want to do several sections in a day, they can. For everyone, though, breaking things down allows the material to be more easily digested; if everything was handed out all at once, at the beginning of the course, the consensus is that students would be overwhelmed. In order to strike a nice balance between the two poles of "not enough" and "too much," some teachers suggest posting two to three weeks of work on a course site at a time. That way, students can see where they have been and where they are headed, and the students who want to work ahead will not get too far ahead.

Profile of a Successful Online Teacher

- Devotes time and energy to teaching online
- Is available to students
- Is creative and willing to experiment
- Breaks down curricula into clearly organized, clearly explained smaller units
- Focuses on concepts, not class periods
- Integrates curricula

Of all the educational developments in the last century, online learning may be the one with the most potential to radically transform our education system. Indeed, significant changes are already underway to accommodate online learning—changes that touch everything, including the way education is funded, delivered, and measured. In numerous areas, online learning is challenging traditional education structures, and the resulting reforms are likely to have implications for decades to come.

At the most basic level, online learning challenges ideas about when, where, and how kids learn best. With the ability to log in anywhere, anytime, and from any place, students and families have experienced freedoms and choices that they will not now easily surrender.

Likewise, as more online programs offer flexibility in how fast or slow students are allowed to proceed through a course, the old mandate to start everyone in September and finish them by May seems increasingly arbitrary. As learning objects become the norm, thus allowing educators to use prescriptive tools that allow them to customize a lesson or an entire course to the specific learning style and needs of each student, a one-size-fits-all approach is also becoming outmoded.

> Online learning is also attacking access and equity issues. Quality curriculum and outstanding teachers are no longer limited to wealthy suburbs or expensive private schools. Internet-based instruction provides access to all students, no matter where they live or what their income.
>
> Finally, online learning is ratcheting up expectations for teacher performance and accessibility. Learning is no longer about creating schedules that are convenient for the teacher or for a bus schedule. In online learning, time centers around learning. If students are working on their lessons at night, why not provide teachers to optimize that learning time?

One of the other major aspects that is benefitted through online education is student choice. Throughout our courses, students are given choices as to how they would like to be assessed. This allows students to utilize Web 2.0 tools to the degree that they are comfortable. Many teachers also facilitate book talks, debates, and discussions all via an online meeting room.

Focuses on Concepts, Not Class Periods

For the teacher, the smaller units can really prove to be a benefit. Because an online teacher is no longer constrained by 45- or 50-minute class periods, he or she is free to focus on concepts, not classroom time. Furthermore, because everything is broken down so completely, it becomes easier to let students know how they are doing in a class.

Integrates Curricula

As teachers break the curricula down into small, well-organized units, they must also work to harness the power of hyperlinking on the Web. The fact that documents can be effortlessly linked together—coupled with the Web's ability to integrate text, images, sounds, and video—means that integrated curriculum, both in terms of content and presentation, is a necessity. Students working online generally dislike straight text-based assignments.

Teacher Training

For teachers to learn how to teach online, they need to receive training. Utah is currently in the midst of training every teacher in the state to be computer literate. EHS teachers are given additional training so that they may effectively teach in that environment. VHS also provides special training for its teachers. Every VHS instructor and site coordinator is required to complete one of the professional development opportunities offered by VHS. These opportunities include either the 10-week, 6 graduate credit NetCourse Instructional Methodologies or the 22-week, 12 graduate credit Teachers' Learning Conference (TLC). These programs cover everything from educational technologies to educational reform. As part of the process, teachers begin creating the course they will be offering through VHS. By the time they finish, they understand how to build and run their own Internet course. Academy On-line also used virtual learning for its teachers as a means of preparing them to teach online; however, it emphasized peer training and support as a key training element. In fact, peer-to-peer training is a strong advantage of teaching online. Teachers can share their materials and collaborate in a more fluid and timely manner with online teaching. In addition to initial training, ongoing staff development is crucial. After all, the Internet changes all the time, so schools must help their teachers keep up.

> **Preparing to Teach Online**
>
> • Virtual High School
>   "A Day in the Life" of an online student
>   http://www.govhs.org/Content/
>   Welcome-VHSLife
>
> • Mind Edge
>   Take an online course
>   http://www.mindedge.com

Positive Consequences of Teaching Online

One of the unexpected results of teaching online is the positive impact that it can have on a teacher's skill in the brick and mortar classroom. Droste related a comment one VHS teacher made to him: "It changed the way I teach my other classrooms. I used to be a talking head, but now I realize that the students have things to offer too." Lillian Bonekin couldn't agree more. Her experience online has made her a more effective teacher all around. "It has helped me in the traditional setting, too, having to be so specific in what I want, writing it down, looking at it, and reviewing it," she explains. "It's helped me see my weaknesses, which sometimes I would take for granted that students already knew something. Now I explain exactly what I want, exactly what my expectations are, so that [the students] are comfortable from the very beginning. I've really improved in that area."

INDIVIDUAL COURSES: SUPPORTING LEARNING

As more homes, housing projects, and community centers plug into high-speed connections, the time and place of learning will become more flexible. Until now, the homeschooling market has had to piece together curriculum and services from many different vendors. As universities such as Texas Tech, MIT, and Stanford, as well as many companies, provide entire courses over the Web, we will see a boom in families making decisions for learning that were once the prerogative of the schools. Parents can and are increasingly purchasing individual courses online to optimize their children's educational opportunities from private companies, such as Apex Learning.

As our schools build the frameworks that link our teachers and students to the world, there will be increasing opportunities to redefine who makes important decisions. For example, teachers can plan their own staff development with Web-based resources. Very exciting work is emerging in Florida and Canada, where teachers are empowered to design new community-based, "one room" high schools that provide more support and personal connections for students who get lost in the traditional high school.

While the flexibility of delivering learning anywhere and at anytime may be perceived as a threat to schools, it can also be viewed as an historic opportunity to build schools that are designed to be smaller, more intimate, and more efficient. For example, there will no longer be a need to have a critical mass of students to offer an advanced placement (AP) calculus course. Ironically, online learning allows us to revisit the best ideas of the one-room schoolhouse. As it has done for other businesses, the Internet may free our best and most creative thinkers to build schools that are not hemmed in by the traditional boundaries of time and space and fixed roles. It is a very exciting time to be in education. Our only limit is our imagination.

Building Online Learning Environments

While there are many institutions and companies dedicated to providing students with online learning experiences, many run their courses with costly and/or custom built software that provides content and fosters interaction among students. Some schools, however, are simply choosing to integrate online learning opportunities into the more traditional brick and mortar school environment. For them, a custom built solution is not always the most cost effective one. Their challenge becomes finding the necessary tools to do this.

BUILDING ON EXCEPTIONAL PROGRAMS

As with any pioneering venture, there will be some failures. Perhaps especially instructive is what became of Alberta's Academy On-line. Academy

On-line, like all other changes to the status quo, took vision and courage to undertake. It also took people who are passionate about education to pioneer such an initiative. Like many pioneers and leaders, they never quite made it to the Promised Land. "Innovative ventures in our schools, such as Academy On-Line, became victims of internal district strife and ceased to operate," Dr. Altha M. Neilson, former Superintendent of Schools in the district that started Academy On-line, explained. "Unfortunately, in order to become stable and accepted, educational initiatives need nurture and support. When that was gone, the initiatives rapidly dwindled or were chopped by the new administration who wanted a quick return to doing things the way they had always been done" (Neilson, 2001). While Academy On-line itself did not survive into the 21st century, more than 26 online schools are now currently operating in Alberta, most of which were inspired by the pioneering educators' efforts. Academy On-line is dead, but the virtual school lives on.

In addition, two broad pieces of advice might be helpful. First of all, the former head of Academy On-line, Wayne Poncia, insists that "every Academy On-line should look different, depending upon the community's needs." This is imperative. Each school has a different group of learners to educate, and it must never lose sight of that. Add to that Bruce Droste's statement: "We weren't techies putting this together, we were educators." As schools look to help their students, they need to forget the technology and focus on the education. The technology will come. It is the teachers, the ideas, and the vision behind the project that will determine its success or failure.

PROFESSIONAL GROWTH OPPORTUNITY

Relate and Reflect on Chapter 5

The following questions are intended to further promote discussion about learning in planning boards, department meetings, school board meetings, and inservice preparation. They do not require any technological skill or expertise to answer. Space is provided after each question so that you may begin to answer them here. Remember that there is no right or wrong answer.

- If online learning is a lifelong skill, should every high school student be required to take the equivalent of an online course?

- Should all teachers be encouraged to create online activities for students within traditional classrooms?

- Should all teachers be encouraged to continue their professional development over the Web?

- Should districts develop their own online courses or, similar to textbooks, purchase online content from a range of vendors?

- If Professor Christensen is correct, and half of all high school courses will be delivered online by 2019, what impact would that have on the allocation of resources in your district?

Appendix

WEB SITES

Chapter 1

Alan November—November Learning **http://www.novemberlearning.com**
Alta Vista Search Engine Home Page **http://www.altavista.com**
American Library Association **http://www.ala.org/**
Answers.com Search Engine **http://www.answers.com**
Ask.com Search Engine **http://www.ask.com**
Climate Change Kids Site **http://www.epa.gov/climatechange/kids/index.html**
EPA Climate Change Home Page **http://www.epa.gov/climatechange**
Federal Bureau of Investigation Kids & Youth Site **http://www.fbi.gov/fbikids.htm**
Global Warming Information Page **http://www.globalwarming.org**
Global Warming International Center Home Page **http://www.globalwarming.net**
Google Search Engine **http://www.google.com**
Home Web Page of Arthur R. Butz **http://pubweb.acns.nwu.edu/~abutz/index.html**
Hotbot Search Engine **http://www.hotbot.com**
MartinLutherKing.org **http://www.martinlutherking.org**
Mid-Continent Regional Educational Laboratory Educator Resources **http://www.mcrel.org/**
Northwestern University **http://www.nwu.edu**
Noodletools Search Engine **http://www.noodletools.com**
November Learning Information Literacy Resources **http://novemberlearning.com/resources/information-literacy-resources/**
Professor Butz's Site via The Wayback Machine **http://web.archive.org/web/20030418061633/http://pubweb.acns.nwu.edu/~abutz/index.html**
Register.com: Domain name registration services **http://www.register.com**
Safe Kids **http://www.safekids.com**
Stormfront Discussion Thread That Includes Arthur Butz **http://www.stormfront.org/forum/showthread.php?t=92404**
United States Holocaust Memorial Museum Home Page **http://www.ushmm.org/museum/exhibit/online/phistories/**
The Wayback Machine **http://www.archive.org**

University of Southern Maine Checklist for Evaluating Web Resources **http://library.usm.maine.edu/research/researchguides/webeval.php**
White Nationalist Links Home Page **http://www.crusader.net/resources/links.html**
Wired Safety **http://www.wiredsafety.org**
Yahoo Search Engine **http://www.yahoo.com**

Chapter 2

AllAfrica.com Home Page **http://www.allafrica.com**
BBC News Online Home Page **http://bbc.co.uk**
ePals **http://www.epals.com**
Facebook **http://www.facebook.com**
Global School House **http://www.globalschoolnet.org**
MySpace **http://www.myspace.com**
Skype **http://www.skype.com**
Thinkquest—**http://www.thinkquest.org/en**
Thinkquest: Library of Entries **http://www.thinkquest.org/pls/html/think.library**
Wikipedia Entry for Videoconferencing—**http://en.wikipedia.org/wiki/Video conferencing**
Worldwide Classroom **http://www.worldwide.edu/travel_planner/pen_pals.html**

Chapter 3

4Teachers Home Page **http://www.4teachers.org**
The Concord Consortium Home Page **http://www.concord.org**
Congressional Record Online **http://www.gpoaccess.gov/crecord/index.html**
Fast Company Home Page **http://www.fastcompany.com**
Linking with Legislators Home Page **http://alpha.musenet.org:81/community/call_stories/story_madison.html**
OpenCongress **http://www.opencongress.org**
Red Herring Home Page **http://www.redherring.com**
Thomas Legislative Information on the Internet Site **http://thomas.loc.gov**
United States House of Representatives **http://www.house.gov**
United States Senate **http://www.senate.gov**

Chapter 4

The American Presidency Project **http://www.presidency.ucsb.edu/showdebate.php?debateid=3**
FirstGov Home Page **http://www.usa.gov/**
The Digital Classroom of the National Archives **http://www.archives.gov/education**
The Internet Archive (Audio of Kennedy/Nixon debate) **http://www.archive.org/audio/xspf_player.php?collectionid=Kennedy-Nixon_third_debate_10_13_1960**

National Archives and Records Administration: Document Analysis **http://www .archives.gov/education/lessons**

National Archives: Establishing an Archive **http://www.archives.gov/about/ history/building-an-archives/school-archives.html**

Chapter 5

Apex Learning Home Page **http://www.apexlearning.com**

Class.com **http://www.class.com**

Electronic High School (EHS) **http://ehs.uen.org**

The Florida Virtual School (FLVS) **http://www.flvs.net/**

GLOW **http://www.ltscotland.org.uk/glowscotland/index.asp**

Illinois Virtual High School (IVHS) **http://www.ivhs.org**

ITunes U **http://www.apple.com/education/mobile-learning/**

Mind Edge **http://www.mindedge.com**

Monterey Institute for Technology and Education **http://www.monterey institute.org**

The Virtual High School (VHS) **http://www.govhs.org**

The Virtual High School: A Day in the Life **http://www.govhs.org/Content/ Welcome-VHSLife**

Bibliography

Armstrong, A., & Casement, C. (2000). *The child and the machine: How computers put our children's education at risk*. Beltsville, MD: Robins Lane Press.

Bridges, W. (1995). *Job shift: How to prosper in a workplace without jobs*. Cambridge, MA: Perseus.

Christensen, C., Horn, M. B., & Johnson, C. W. (2008). *Disrupting class: How disruptive innovation will change the way the world learns*. New York: McGraw-Hill.

Csikszentmihalyi, M. (1991). *Flow: The psychology of optimal experience*. New York: HarperPerennial.

D'Amico, C. (1997). *Workforce 2000 revisited: Work and workers in the 21st century*. Indianapolis, IN: Hudson Institute.

Davis, S., & Botkin, J. (1994). *The monster under the bed*. New York: Simon & Schuster.

Davis, S., & Meyer, C. (1998). *Blur: The speed of change in the connected economy*. Reading, MA: Addison-Wesley.

Disessa, A. A. (2000). *Changing minds: Computers, learning, and literacy*. Cambridge: Massachusetts Institute of Technology (MIT) Press.

Edwards, C. M. (1995). The Internet high school: A modest proposal. *National Association of Secondary School Principals (NASSP) Bulletin, 79*(573), 67–71.

Gardner, H. (1993). *Multiple intelligences: The theory in practice*. New York: Basic Books.

Henderson, A. T., & Berla, N. (Eds.). (1994). *A new generation of evidence: The family is critical to student achievement*. Washington, DC: National Committee for Citizens in Education.

Jenkins, L. (1998). *Improving student learning: Applying Deming's quality principles in classrooms*. Milwaukee, WI: American Society for Quality (ASQ) Press.

Kurshan, B., Morse, G., & November, A. (1993). *Understanding computers through applications/student resource*. New York: Glencoe/McGraw-Hill.

Lazear, D. (1994). *Seven pathways of learning: Teaching students and parents about multiple intelligences*. Tucson, AZ: Zephyr Press.

Mandel, S. (1999). *Virtual field trips in the cyberage: A content mapping approach*. Arlington Heights, IL: SkyLight.

Minsky, M. (1988). *The society of the mind*. New York: Simon & Schuster.

National Education Association. (2002). *Guide to online high school courses*. Retrieved January 29, 2008, from http://www.nea.org/home/30113.htm

Norman, D. A. (1990). *The design of everyday things*. New York: Currency/Doubleday.

Postman, N. (1993). *Technopoly: The surrender of culture to technology.* New York: Vintage Books.

Postman, N. (1996). *The end of education: Redefining the value of school.* New York: Alfred A. Knopf.

Rinehart, G. (1993). *Quality education: Applying the philosophy of Dr. W. Edwards Deming to transform the educational system.* New York: McGraw-Hill.

Salomon, G., Perkins, D. N., & Globerson, T. (1991). Partners in cognition: Extending human intelligence with intelligent technologies. *Educational Researcher. 20,* 10–16.

Sarason, S. B. (1990). *The predictable failure of educational reform: Can we change course before it's too late?* San Francisco: Jossey-Bass.

Senge, P. M. (1990). *The fifth discipline: The art and practice of the learning organization.* New York: Doubleday Currency.

Steinbeck, J. (1992). *The grapes of wrath.* New York: Penguin Books.

Swift, J. (1995). *A modest proposal and other satires.* Amherst, NY: Prometheus Books.

Tapscott, D. (1996). *The digital economy: Promise and peril in the age of networked intelligence.* New York: McGraw-Hill.

Tapscott, D. (1997). *Growing up digital: The rise of the Net generation.* New York: McGraw-Hill.

Treadwell, M. (1999). *1001 of the best Internet sites for educators.* Arlington Heights, IL: SkyLight.

Turkle, S. (1997). *Life on the screen: Identity in the age of the Internet.* Westport, CT: Touchstone Books.

Weiner, R. S. (2000). Educators' approach to technology funding matures. *New York Times.* Retrieved March, 26, 2001, from http://nytimes.com/2000/11/29/technology/29EDUCATION.html

Wheatley, M. J. (1992). *Leadership and the new science: Learning about organization from an orderly universe.* San Francisco: Berrett-Koehler.

Wheatley, M. J. (1996). *A simpler way.* San Francisco: Berrett-Koehler.

Wirth, A. G. (1992). *Education and work for the year 2000: Choices we face.* San Francisco: Jossey-Bass.

Zuboff, S. (1988). *In the age of the smart machine: The future of work and power.* New York: Basic Books.

Index

CORWIN

A SAGE Company

The Corwin logo—a raven striding across an open book—represents the union of courage and learning. Corwin is committed to improving education for all learners by publishing books and other professional development resources for those serving the field of PreK–12 education. By providing practical, hands-on materials, Corwin continues to carry out the promise of its motto: **"Helping Educators Do Their Work Better."**